LENNY McLEAN

THE

GUV'NOR

A TRIBUTE

LENNY McLEAN

THE

GUV'NOR

A TRIBUTE

Peter Gerrard

BLAKE

Published by Blake Publishing Ltd,
3 Bramber Court, 2 Bramber Road
London W14 9PB, England

First Published in Hardback in 2000

ISBN 185782 3974

British Library Cataloguing-in-Publication Data:

A catalogue record for this book is available from the British Library.

Designed by GDAdesign

Printed in Great Britain by Creative Print and Design (Wales),
Ebbw Vale, Gwent.

3 5 7 9 10 8 6 4 2

Pictures reproduced by kind permission of the *East London Advertiser*,
Simon Fowler, Gabor Scott, Don Barrett and Camera Press.
Every attempt has been made to contact the copyright-holders,
but some were unobtainable. We would be grateful if the
relevant people would contact us.

Lenny McLean
The Guv'nor

Contents

CHAPTER I

A Tribute to Lenny
by Peter Gerrard

SINCE PUBLICATION of *The Guv'nor* – Lenny McLean's autobiography – in June 1998, it has never been out of one chart or another. Number one bestseller, best autobiography of 1998 – eighth best a full year later and still selling like hot-cakes. A phenomenal success that has overtaken the books of such people as Richard Branson, David Attenborough, John Major and other names known the world over.

Feedback told us that throughout the world someone somewhere was reading the book. On a Concord flight to New York, a beach in Tangier, Golf Club in Hong Kong, poolside in Spain. This story of one man's struggle to survive and to, in his own words, 'put steam on the table', seemed to grip the public imagination.

I have personally received hundreds of letters and emails posthumously congratulating Lenny, through me, for a read that was both moving and inspiring. These came not only from the length a breadth of the UK, but from places as far flung as Hawaii, Australia, South Africa, Japan and even one from Russia. Almost without exception they asked the question 'What was Lenny really like?' as though they found it hard to believe that he could be really the same character as portrayed in his autobiography. The only reply I could give was that he was exactly as he came over in the book.

With certain characters within this genre, it can take a fair bit of imagination and airbrushing of their lives to paint an acceptable word picture. They loved their mums; they subscribed to *Christian* weekly, loveable rascals all, who in fact were innocent victims of the murder and mayhem they were guilty of. This was not the case with Lenny. I can't say that what you saw is what you got, because in his case if you only knew the public face you could only have the impression of an unbeatable fighter, a hard case – a man as tough and unbending as he looked. But you would only be seeing one part of his many sides. Violence and intimidation when called for was Lenny's work. Most of the time he hated what he had to do, but it was something that was thrust upon him and he accepted that it brought bread into the house and gave his family everything they could want. Which he often said was what his life was all about.

Many things set him apart from the stereotypical tough guy who could have a fight, but three things stand out. His very sharp mind, a protective instinct for the underdog and, above all else, an infectious sense of humour.

He was no academic, but then this has never been a mark of anyone's intelligence, of which Len had more than the average. In a sense this was a secret weapon, for anyone deluded enough to presume he was just another grunting thug would get a very rude awakening indeed – whether an opponent, a chancer or someone taking him on in a business deal. Nothing got past him. He could read whoever he met in a matter of minutes and though he didn't always act on what he saw, that person would be compartmentalised into friend, foe or of 'no value' very quickly. Once established as a friend you'd be under the Guv'nor's wing for life – anything less and everything you said after that would be mentally taken apart as he established in his own mind what your angle was or how you were trying to graft him. The subtlety of it was that on the outside he never gave a clue as to what was going on inside. He often said, 'Peter, some people never learn that they can't graft a grafter – I'm always ten steps in front of them.'

One of the few other people I met who were gifted in this way was Ronnie Kray. His eyes, like Lenny's, never left yours in a conversation. And many times I sat across from Ronnie on visits to Broadmoor thinking, God help anyone who thinks they can lie or flannel this man. He seemed to look right inside your head. In a way with Ronnie that was chilling, though I never felt that with Len, even if the end result was the same.

Unless you had been on the end of a right hander, it was his humour, if nothing else, by which you would remember him. Nothing, apart from work, was too serious or too sacred for him not to break into some sort of joke. These were not of the 'Did you hear about the nun and the bishop' variety, but more clever and very funny observations on the people and things that were going on around him. Many of these, though, were 'in jokes' which left others puzzling as to what was so funny. Though he could put on a menacing face at the drop of a hat, it is that grin of his and that laugh, as big as the man himself, which will always stay in the minds of those who knew him.

As for his capacity for looking after, or at least wanting to look after, the interests of those he saw as weaker than himself (a category most of us would fall into), it was an integral part of his character. He seemed to take it personally that there were slags out there that could mug old ladies, abuse little babies and sell drugs to schoolkids. He'd read such news out of the paper and fume with anger – 'If I got my hands on them fuckers I'd rip them to pieces.' Sometimes he did – other times he passed the word on to people in a better position to right a wrong. But he couldn't take on everyone's problems as much as he wanted to.

Along with a number of others in our village we were burgled. Everyone including the police knew who the two men were, but as often happens in these cases the hands of the law were tied. When my wife Shirley happened to mention this to Lenny he was outraged – absolutely beside himself with anger that anyone should dare to rob friends of his. He said to her, 'Don't go away from that phone, I'll be back in two minutes.' One minute later he was telling her that first thing next morning we were to expect two very large fellas to turn up on our doorstep.

'All you got to do is tell them where those dogs live and leave the rest to them – you ain't involved.'

Fortunately for the thieves they were arrested later that day in an unrelated incident and subsequently were given sentences of two years. If they'd known what punishment Len had arranged for them I'm sure they would have considered prison as the easier option. Lenny's immediate reaction that day brought home to us both exactly what he meant when he said, 'You're under my wing.'

You only had to meet Lenny once and it would stay with you for the rest of your life. I've often tried to understand what special something he had but have never quite pinned it down. A lot of people imagine meeting Lenny would be akin to meeting someone like Mike Tyson – big tough guy, and there it ends. But they would be wrong, as there was so much more to him than physique. If you had something to say he listened and took every word in. Too many of us must have come across somebody of importance who hogs the conversation with self-self-self, then when it's someone else's turn to get a word in the shutters come down and their eyes glaze over. Not with Len. He made you feel he was genuinely interested in what you had to say, which he was. He'd got no time for arse-lickers or bullshitters, even though he'd listen politely, but you could always see that he'd got their mark.

Time and time again I'd be with Lenny when he'd be accosted by someone or other that had known him in prison. Invariably they'd all be cast in the same mould,

Once established as a friend, you'd be under the Guv'nor's wing for life. Lenny is shown here with his 'book man', Peter Gerrard tattooed from arseholes to breakfast time and wearing fistfuls of sovereigns. 'Hey Big Lenny, remember me? B wing, I used to slop out for you.'

Down would come the eyebrows. 'Bill, ain't it?'

'No Len, it's Fred.'

'Course it is, but you look just like Bill. Good to see you pal – how they treating you? All right for a bit of scratch?' A handshake and a 'Mind how you go' sent off whoever it was, buzzing with pride that the Guv'nor remembered him from all those years back. Out of sight, Lenny would say to me 'Who was that c–t? Now do you see those sort of people I want to get away from? I don't want to be involved with them, I don't want them knocking on my door and getting near my family and I don't want to speak to them.' But the point I'm making is that he *had* spoken to them, and with a polite friendliness that cost him nothing but left the other fella feeling good.

Success breeds jealousies and no exception was made when Lenny's book took the publishing world by storm. Remember that apart from everything else this man was first and foremost a father, a husband and loyal friend of many. His family was in mourning, yet this didn't prevent one journalist from suggesting that Lenny's death was the greatest publicity stunt ever. He knows who he is and he's nothing but scum. Another printed that Lenny died through taking drugs and steroids. No basis in fact at all, but no doubt it made this obviously failed author feel he was man of the moment as he attacked someone whose boots he wasn't fit to clean.

A spokesman for one of the country's top publishers,

a company who to their everlasting regret rejected Len's story, rubbished the thousands of book buyers in a fit of pique by describing them as 'upwardly mobile white trash'. Yet I know for a fact that those people who read and were knocked out by the book came from all walks of society. These pathetic critics and others are beneath contempt so I shouldn't let them get to me. Perhaps I should think of what Len is saying as he's looking down: 'They ain't no value son – Fuck 'em.'

The saddest part of this phenomenal success is that he died one day before his book rocketed to the number one slot, where it was to stay for two months. This was Lenny's dream and the thought of seeing his life in print kept him going in those last months of his life. Yet only he could say why it was so important to him, and he never did.

Surprisingly, for a man who had overcome obstacles that would have flattened mere mortals like ourselves, become the best in the business and above all gained respect from everyone who knew him, occasionally he needed reassurance that he was what he was. He didn't ask this of his public – they got what was expected – the big tough guy exuding confidence. But away from the limelight he often asked, 'How am I doing? How do I look?' And as far as the book was concerned, particularly nearing publication, he would often ask, 'What do you think Peter? Is this going to be a bestseller? Will it be better than all the rest?' I had enormous faith in his book and had from the beginning, but I could no more predict a bestseller than I could the winning lottery numbers. Nevertheless, I'd assure him that we'd be way up there with the best and he'd be happy with that until the next time doubts crept in.

I suppose that for anyone to have their life set out for posterity between two hard covers is the ultimate accolade. It means you've arrived, and this is what it must have meant to Lenny. He'd be the first to admit he wasn't an educated man. He'd never needed writing skills and his spelling was not good at all, which reminds me of a time someone asked me to get a signed photograph of Len. I gave it to him and he said 'Go on then, what shall I put?'

I said, ' Just write To Neil, all the best ...'

'OK, how do I spell that?'

Letter by letter I said 'N.E.I.L.' then without thinking carried on 'A.L.L.'

He growled, flung the pen down and gave me a look saying, 'I ain't that bad, I can spell ALL you c—t.' He saw the funny side of it though.

He was no exception amongst people who'd had no real formal education. Books were a mystery and something special, and those who had their name on one were set above everyone else. That's what Len wanted – nothing to do with vanity but simply to prove to everyone that an East End boy could get right to the top

Though the book had been written and finished shortly after we met, it was to be years of setbacks and frustrations before it saw the light of day. In Len's words everyone who got involved in either the book or the film had led us down 'the happy road'. Meaning too many arseholes in suits had been telling us what they thought we wanted to hear, but always projecting their promises – next month, next year. Len was getting more disillusioned by a business world that couldn't or wouldn't make decisions with the speed that he always conducted anything that needed to be done.

If he was asked to do a bit of work – a favour or a phone call, it was done there and then. No excuses, no promises for next week – it was done immediately. He thought he should be shown the same respect, but unfortunately in businesses most decisions are made by committee, and it never happened.

So no wonder when years later he held his book for the first time he said to me, 'This is one of the best days of my life.' I'll always carry a picture in my mind of him sitting there with a copy on his knee, grinning and thoughtfully nodding his head. I felt privileged for having been instrumental in bringing about this moment for him. Privileged that I could repay a debt to this man who never asked for anything, never kept a note of favours done and spent so much of his time helping to push others up the ladder, accepting nothing in return.

But back at the turn of 1998 he was feeling pissed off in general with lack of any concrete interest in either book or film and an ongoing cold didn't help make him feel any better.

Early February Len and Val took off for a holiday in Spain and two days after they left John Blake agreed to publish *The Guv'nor* in the Autumn of that year. Not wanting to give Len reason for another disappointment I hadn't mentioned that I had been in contact with Blake's

small publishing house. Now after a day or so in negotiation a deal was agreed and the big fella was out of the country so I couldn't let him know. The remainder of that fortnight seemed like a year, as I couldn't wait to give him the news.

When he rang me after the holiday his voice sounded a bit flat – not like himself at all. What I didn't know at that time was that the trip to Spain had not gone well. He'd felt weak and tired and wished he'd never gone. Still, I was going to cheer him up. I said, 'Len I've got good news and bad news – how do you want it?'

He thought for a minute and said, 'Gimme the bad.'

I said, 'Len, the upfront deal is shit – the good news is we're going to get your book published this year.'

All he said was, 'Fuck me. I don't believe it.' There was a long pause then like he'd had a shot of adrenaline and the old Lenny was back on the line. 'Good boy – set up a meet – never mind the money, that'll come later. We're on the way, nothing's going to stop us now.'

With the cruellest irony possible a few weeks later Lenny was diagnosed with cancer. Four short months later this humorous giant, this invincible man, was to die at the age of forty-nine without knowing the impact his life would have on thousands of ordinary people.

After that phone call, when I felt at last I was repaying a great debt to Len, I made a visit to see him at his home in Bexleyheath. We sat in his conservatory smoking, drinking tea and talking about this and that. About

Left: If he was asked to do a bit of work – a favour or a phone call – it was done immediately.

lunchtime he suggested we drove into the East End so he could get a haircut. It seemed just another day – but it wasn't. In himself Lenny seemed his usual self – snatches of song, a joke, droll comments on passers by. But when we parked up and walked to the barber shop, I couldn't help noticing two things. One was that he was throwing his foot slightly with every step and the other was that he kept veering into me. Possibly the only reason I noticed this was that it reminded me of my own father after he'd suffered a minor stroke.

Haircut out of the way we headed home and it was the most erratic and nerve-wracking journey I'd ever had with Lenny. Usually he drove his black Mercedes nice and sedately, but that day he hit top speeds through the town, braking at junctions with inches to spare behind the car in front. When we pulled into traffic on the Blackwell Tunnel approach without stopping my heart was in my mouth. What was I going to say, 'Fuck's sake Len, slow down'? He'd only recently bothered to get a driving licence but he'd been driving for well over thirty years. I just thought he was preoccupied. That was the last journey we were to make together with Len behind the wheel. I can't say that in any way this was a sign to me of things to come, but it gave me pause for thought and I remember getting home and saying to my wife that I thought there was something wrong with Lenny.

Shortly after this we had our lunch with John Blake and, showman that he was, Len rose to the occasion no matter how he felt inside. Len knew what he was and knew the sort of impression he could make on anyone who met him. For three hours he kept us and surrounding tables entertained with his stories. A slight downside, though not obvious to anyone who didn't know him well, was that he forgot the punchline of many of these stories. Invariable I knew the ending and all it took was a word to put him back on track. When it was new to me I had no choice but to leave him floundering and I could see the frustration in his face.

What none of us would know for some time was that Len was keeping to himself the fact that he was going through what he would later describe as having bells going off in his head. Angry at what he must have thought as an uncharacteristic weakness on his part, he verbally lashed out at me. When John left the table for a few minutes he said, 'Fuck's sake Peter – don't just sit there, you've got to help me out. You're making me look a mug in front of people.' The criticism was unreasonable as Lenny's bollockings often were, but equally they were forgotten in minutes.

One such bollocking that sticks in my mind was when we drove to a meeting in London. We left Len's motor in a seven-storey car park. When we came back for it some hours later we couldn't find the car. We searched up and down the level we thought it was on, then Len said 'You go up, I'll go down and we'll soon spot it.' Off we went. At first all I could hear was Len's footsteps echoing up. I looked over the balcony and could see him strolling along without a care in the world. He broke into 'Carolina Moon', stopping every now and then to call up,

'Found my motor yet?'

'No, Len.'

'Good boy – keep looking.'

This went on for a quarter of an hour and I could tell he was starting to get the hump because the singing had given way to muttering and 'Fuck's sakes'. Then he started to lecture me – bearing in mind that I was three flights above his head. Fortunately the multi-storey was deserted. 'You know what your trouble is?' He wasn't interested in an answer. 'You know what your trouble is? You've got too much country air up your nose. You live out in the sticks and don't know what life's about. HOW THE FUCK CAN YOU LOSE MY MOTOR?' I looked over the edge again and watched him walking along and talking to me as though I was beside him. 'Sometimes, Peter, I think your brain is no bigger than a walnut.' And as he spoke he stretched each word out twice as long as it needed to be. 'BUT – I don't blame you, I blame myself for thinking you was capable of finding that fucking great motor.' He went on in the same vein until checking one of the levels he'd been searching; there was his car – just where he'd parked it. Did he apologise and say it was his own fault that he couldn't remember where the car was? Nope.

Some miles down the road he said, 'You know I had to bollock you back there, don't you? You're not streetwise and I have to straighten you out.' And it was all forgotten. He was six years my junior, yet he acted like a father – not just to me but most people he had contact with. Maybe it was down to a lifestyle that crammed every year full of more

26

excitement and events than an ordinary man might see in a lifetime, but he was always much older than his years.

Reg Kray said Lenny was a man born out of his time, and that hit it on the head, for everything about him was a throwback to the old time Guv'nors. Those men who ruled and held together manors by the sheer force of not only their strength but of their larger-than-life

Below: Reg Kray said Lenny was a man born out of his time, and that hit it on the head, for everything about him was a throwback to the old time Guv'nors.

personalities. Men to whom respect, family and code of conduct was what made life worthwhile. Men who had virtually disappeared by the sixties only to be remembered as legends.

Perhaps heredity had something to do with the way Lenny was. You don't have to look any further than his great uncle Jimmy Spinks to see a mirror of what Lenny was to become in more modern times. Seven inches shorter than Lenny, he was massively built with barrel chest and powerful arms, neck and shoulders. Like his nephew he had no time or need for weapons – his fists were enough. To quote Reggie again, 'Anyone taking Spinks on had to resort to blades and iron bars to compensate for their own inadequacy.' Hence the tramline scars that marred his rugged good looks. Again mirroring what was to come, such was his reputation and fearsome build, an American producer offered him the chance to be taken to the States to appear in the movies. He turned the offer down, unlike Lenny, who when given the chance to get into the acting game by Paul Knight, grabbed it with both hands – grateful, as he put it, to leave behind the violence and dealings with 'no value low life' to make a new life with 'proper people' for his Val and the kids.

Going back to that meeting, I know there are two incidents that must stick in John Blake's mind, aside from the sheer impact of meeting Lenny for the first time. As we left Leonardo's in the Kings Road Len said, 'Hold up John, I wanna show you these,' and without more ado pulled down the back of his trousers and showed off his

Above: **Lenny shows Craig Fairbrass what it takes to be the Guv'nor.**

bullet-scarred backside. I'd seen him pull this stunt a number of times and it was an example of his wicked humour. He knew the shock value of the old scars, particularly as they were caused by a shotgun, something ordinary people never see in a lifetime, and where he showed them off – in this case on the pavement – added to the moment.

The other incident happened when we left John outside the restaurant and crossed the road. He hailed a taxi, one of thousands in London, and as he sat in the back the driver said to him, 'See that big fella over there,' pointing across the road, 'that's Lenny McLean, the Guv'nor.' Any doubt John might have had as to whether this book he'd taken on was about some little-known fighter vanished immediately.

Since that day I've often wondered whether Lenny had some unconscious premonition of what was to come. We'd had meetings before where we'd been led to believe that either the book or the film was tied up and ready to go, when in fact we were being led down 'the happy road', without knowing it at the time. In ignorance of the fact that what we had been discussing would end up in another let-down, Lenny would talk non-stop all the way home, full of enthusiasm and plans for the future.

After our lunch with John Blake, even though a contract was signed and sealed he seemed sunk in thought. Minutes after we got into the taxi he put his arm round my shoulder saying 'We're on the way son. Now we're in the driving seat.' Then he lapsed into silence for the rest of the twenty-five minute journey. Just sat with his arm round me, occasionally patting me on the shoulder. I'm still moved by the thought even now. This was a high point in his life. At last he could reach out and grasp that dream. Same for myself really, for chasing publication of our book, which we both believed in, had been a large part of both our lives for years.

As far as we were concerned things could only get better and better.

A matter of weeks later Lenny was admitted to hospital for tests. He covers this short period simply, but dramatically, in the final chapter of his book. What appeared to be a case on ongoing flu or a bronchial infection was suddenly out in the open as terminal cancer. Out of hospital Lenny rang my wife Shirley at seven thirty in the morning. 'Shell,' he said, 'they've given me four months to a year to live but I'll show 'em.' Devastated, she cried her way through the conversation with him telling her that she's got to be strong, as though the diagnosis was the other way round. Later on it was my turn to speak to him and I dreaded making the call. What can you say to someone facing their own end in such a short time? When he answered the telephone I got so choked up with emotion that all I could say was, 'Len.' When you know someone well words aren't needed. My silence said what I felt, and his that he understood. Then he said, 'Right, never mind all that, me and you have got work to do with the book.' Never mind all that – what more would you expect from the Guv'nor?

In his book he himself says he wouldn't go into the pain, the tears and heartbreak suffered within his very close family, and it's not my place to do so either. I will say that it was Lenny's personal strength that got everyone who knew him through the next four painful months. Any enquiry as to how he felt was met with, 'Top of the world. Strong as a bull.' And he was.

Thankfully we didn't have the added pain of seeing this big man fade into nothingness, as often happens with this illness. You could see pain in his eyes, but that wasn't for himself, it was for Val and his kids. A weak leg gave him a slight limp, but apart from that his public face was the same old Lenny.

The book was scheduled for autumn publication, but many things have to be taken into consideration prior to the day. Printing, distribution, advertising, publicity, all have to slot in place, otherwise it's chaos.

Len totally accepted the way things might turn out, but on the other hand still held on to stories of so and so's uncle who'd been given six months and was still fit and healthy ten years later. It happens, and we all prayed for some miracle. Realistically though, my wife, Val and myself felt that as it was so important to Lenny, rather than take any chances we'd ask for the date to be brought forward, and John Blake, bending the strict rules of publishing agreed it would hit the bookshops in July. That this would cause a few problems was nothing compared to giving Len the very thing he was focusing on.

One thing that caused us concern was that book-signing and TV appearances might be too much for him in his weakened state. But he was all for it, saying, 'I don't care if I have to crawl on my hands and knees or be carried on a stretcher, I'm going to do everything I have to do as long as it helps the book.'

In those last weeks, as we waited for these various dates to come up, Lenny and I had a lot of conversations about life and the possibility of his own death. Not once did he ask 'Why me?' or complain about the hand he'd been dealt. Only once did he actually voice any regret, and even that was said with humour. With Len you didn't feel as though you had to choose your words or pretend things were normal. So, without thinking, I said to him

32

that it was Shirley's fiftieth birthday in a few months and that, typical for a woman, she wasn't looking forward to it. He laughed and said, 'I wish I was going to see my fiftieth, but there's no chance of that.'

He told me that he believed in incarnation, though he didn't use that word. He said, 'I ain't talking about ghosts or all that cobblers, but I do believe that we all get reborn – could be a butterfly or cat or anything. That's why you should treat every living thing with respect because you never know who that thing might have been in another life.' I asked him what he'd like to come back as. He thought about it then said, 'Don't give a fuck really, just so long as I do come back so I can keep an eye open for my Val.'

He said something to Val one day that was so poignant it hurts even to recall it. He took her hand and said, 'Val, what am I going to do without you?' What was going through his mind when he said it? I won't even try and guess. His thoughts were all of his family but he wasn't forgetting his book man. He'd say, 'Look, I won't be around much longer so I won't be able to look after you, but I'll make sure that if you're ever in trouble there's people you can ring. Another thing, I've had a word here and there so you won't ever be stuck for somebody to write about. And you know if Lenny says he'll do something, it's done.'

And it was. I don't think anyone, apart from Val, Jamie and Kelly, will ever know the superhuman effort that it took for Len to carry on apparently normally. He didn't want to leave his family and he wanted to publicise his book so he forced himself on when anyone lesser would

Above: Lenny said something to Val one day towards the end that was so poignant it hurts even to recall it. He took her hand and said, 'Val, what am I going to do without you?'

Opposite: Lenny always felt it was disrespectful to others not to be smart and tidy, no matter who it was he was meeting, and not once did I ever see him lower his standard. Here he is, as sharply dressed as ever, with Ted 'Kid' Berg, legendary fight promoter Alex Steene, and Charlie Richardson's son and friends.'

have understandably given up the fight.

Though he'd given up tearing about all over the place like he used to, filling his days with business and meets here and there, he still kept up with what was going on by telephone. Even at this stage he was either working or doing a favour by, as he called it, growling down the blower at someone who hadn't paid a debt or was out of order. As ill as he was he never lost the power to intimidate when necessary.

Lenny always felt it was disrespectful to others not to

be smart and tidy, no matter who it was he was meeting, and not once did I ever see him lower that standard. He might not have been leaving the house but no matter when I called on him I never saw him anything other than clean-shaven and smartly dressed.

Again I've got to repeat, did he know that his time was shorter than anyone else could have guessed? We all prayed that he would have many months, but when you're in a situation such as his are you given some unconscious message? I say this because some time

35

before he died we were invited to his home because he wanted to take us all out for lunch. We turned up as agreed at about twelve thirty and as we stood in the hallway Val whispered, ' He's been dressed and sitting there waiting for you since eleven.' Before Val drove us to a local pub, we gave him a couple of wrapped gifts, as it had been his birthday some days previously. Though he was protesting that, 'Nah, you shouldn't have done this,' his obvious pleasure as he tore the paper off was touching. The lunch was just a simple get together, but it stands out in our minds as an oasis during tense and worrying times. Lenny was quiet but relaxed and he talked matter-of-factly about his illness, his book and plans for the future, savouring the moment with his Val and friends. My lingering memory is of the sadness in his eyes behind the humorous banter and of the fact that he didn't want that lunch to end. 'Ain't this nice? Go on, let's have another lemonade.' Just another memory, but one of so many that keeps him alive and larger than life in our heads.

Very shortly before he died I arrived unannounced at his home one afternoon. Val told me that he'd slept solidly from the previous evening and was sorry but it looked like I wouldn't be able to see him. I said not to worry, as I understood how things were, and I'd just drink the cup of tea she was already making then slip away. We talked for about ten minutes then Val looked at me and said, 'Listen.' Suddenly I heard footsteps coming down the stairs followed by that booming voice, 'PEETERRRR my friend.' I could feel my eyes filling up before he even reached the door. A blow of the nose because as he would say, 'Never mind all that,' but I was choked that having heard my voice downstairs there was no way he was going to stay in bed with a guest in the house. I asked him how he felt, though knew the answer before he said, 'Top of the world. Strong as a bull.' Could I have expected any less from my friend?

Shortly after this he was invited to appear on the Richard Littlejohn TV show. This was another occasion where, debilitated by his ongoing illness, he'd slept all day. But an hour before the car arrived to take us to the studios, he was up, suited and booted and ready to put on a show. When we turned up at the studio we were shown into the green room, given food and drinks and introduced to the other guests who were going to appear on the show. There's an expression, 'A man for all men', and that was Lenny.

For the butcher, defying the law and facing prosecution for selling beef on the bone, Len was with him all the way against 'the fucking suits who ain't got a clue about real life'. For a giggling group of four girl singers who were no strangers to a good meal and billed as 'The Fat Spice Girls' he was full of jokes, hugs and kisses – and they loved him. When it came to the mother of Lesley Ann Downey, the child murdered by Ian Brady and Myra Hindley, his compassion was overwhelming, as he held her hand, talked to her quietly for five minutes and finished with a reassuring cuddle.

We had a chat with Littlejohn, who knew Len from previous shows, and as he was walking away Len said,

'Richard, don't forget I want my pal right beside me in front of the cameras.' Richard said he'd have a word with the producer and left the room, just as the most stunning girl walked in.

She was so striking in skin-tight trousers and see-through top that she was pinned to the wall by every male eye in the room. Lenny loved a pretty girl, but unlike the average man I'd never known him to make lewd comments, and this was no exception. We just looked at each other with raised eyebrows, which said it all. She looked around the room then made a beeline for Len and asked him if he would mind if she had a photograph taken with him. We didn't know it then but the time he had left was short, yet that unthreatening charisma hadn't left him one bit. After getting his autograph and a hug that was a knife thrust to every other man in the room, Tara, as she was known, said, 'I'm flying out to meet the President of America next week.'

Lenny laughed and said, 'Well tell him you met the Guv'nor first and he says "Hello".'

With his shot coming up fast Len found out it wasn't possible for me to appear alongside him. Out came the jaw, down went the eyebrows ''Scuse me?' he said to the director. 'This is my book man and if he don't go on nor do I!' He meant it and I loved him for his loyalty, but sticking me between Lenny and Tony Banks, the Minister of Sport, would have confused the issue and wouldn't work. I talked him into accepting the situation and he reluctantly agreed, but only after a compromise was

Opposite: **Every inch the Guv'nor.**

reached where I would be placed in the audience where the cameras could pick me up at a given time. 'Make sure you do,' Len growled, 'cos I want everybody to see the man who's been beside me all the way.'

When he walked towards the stage the applause was deafening. But what a contrast to the appearance he'd made on the same show a few years earlier. Then, as his name was announced, he'd stepped through the curtain, paused for a moment, then raised his arms as if to say, 'Here I am'. With his powerful physique straining against the fabric of an immaculate suit, he seemed at a peak of fitness and health, beaming all over his face and every inch the Guv'nor the audience were waiting for. This time the contrast was painful and emotional. Leaning heavily on a walking stick and with obvious effort, he made his way towards Littlejohn. But don't let me give the impression that he was a pathetic shadow of his former self. Yes he looked older and yes he looked tired, but the quiet dignity of the man was awe-inspiring.

After the initial banter that was typical of Lenny, the audience fell silent as he explained what he was now facing. As he quite matter-of-factly said, 'I've only got a few months to live,' a gasp went round the studio, but he carried on as though what he'd said was of little importance. He didn't need and didn't want sympathy. This cancer was the hand he had been dealt and he was dealing with it in his usual style.

Then the conversation turned to his book, which as usual on these programmes was shown but not actually displayed very prominently. It's a sort of unspoken situation where, yeah you can have a plug but we're not giving you too much free publicity. This is usually accepted by the author rather than rock the boat. Not Lenny though. He picked it up from the desk and with a big grin on his face held it up to the camera and put his thumb up to me in the audience. Did he bask in the singular glory of author? Of course not. He pointed up to me and said, 'This was written by Peter Gerrard – top writer in the country.' The camera swung round, panned in and caught me with a lump in my throat as big as an orange. So what. I don't think there was a dry eye in the studio. As the credits started to roll the audience gave him a standing ovation of cheering and clapping that just went on and on long after we were off the air, showing in the only way they could that they were behind him every inch of the way in this his final battle.

The next goal for Lenny to aim towards was a book signing at a Dillons store in Oxford Street. Val, quite rightly, was concerned that he was overdoing things, what with his other appearances and now this signing, but no way could he be talked out of it. He'd agreed to publicise the book and that was what he was going to do, rising to the occasion every time. Often these signings can be embarrassing affairs. In the two hours set aside for it four people might turn up – two of them buy a book while the other two want an autograph on a scrap of paper. But not when the big fella was behind the table. Well over two hundred people queued round the store and spilled out on to the pavement, and Len had a word for every one of them.

Again, no one but those close to him could tell that

the effort required from him was akin to climbing a mountain. Occasionally his forehead would be beaded with perspiration, and watching him closely I could see sadness and a distance in his eyes. What was he thinking? His strength and courage had brought him further than anyone expected. He'd seen his book published, held that dream in his hands, fulfilled his obligations by appearing to his public – so was he now thinking that he should step back and let things take their course? We'll never know, but that look is a picture I'll always carry in my head, alongside another later that day of him gently cradling my eight-week-old grandson Owen. The hardest man in Britain, an unbeaten streetfighter who'd taken on the Mafia and intimidated the IRA, holding that tiny baby as if it was the most natural thing in the world to do. This was the real Lenny behind the closed door of his home – a gentle man in every sense.

A week later, warned by Val that the doctors had advised her that his time was running short, I drove to Bexleyheath fearing the worst. I know this illness can have a devastating effect on one's appearance in a matter of days and I was apprehensive about how I would find him. I needn't have worried. There he was, same as ever, comfortably seated in his favourite part of the house – the conservatory. Cup of tea and his roll-ups in front of him. I didn't stay long, knowing that though he might not allow it to show, everything he did took great effort and left him very tired. He was full of the next book signing and how this time we'd sell a thousand. He even spoke of what he might do once he got a bit of strength back.

There were film parts in the offing, but he wasn't rushing to take them up until he was completely fit. Listening to his plans tore me apart, knowing that none of them could materialise.

The following Tuesday my wife and I turned up at his home because all week on the phone he'd insisted he was up for another signing session. When we arrived he was upstairs in a deep sleep but had left a message for us with Val. It was to tell Pete and Shell to go in his place and make sure they tell the people that the Guv'nor was a bit off-colour but he'd soon be back on his feet to sign all the books they want. Naturally Val stayed with him while Eddie, a good friend of the family, put himself out to drive us to WHSmiths bookshop at Liverpool Street station. Another fantastic turn out, but this time we had to apologise for Len's absence without making too much of his illness. Instead of being disgruntled or put out that the man they had travelled to see wasn't available, we were given nothing but sympathy and best wishes to pass on to Lenny. This time I signed on his behalf and again hundreds were taken from the shelves.

It had been another very successful day, and to be honest Shirley and I couldn't wait to get back to Bexleyheath and tell Len all about it. We knew it would certainly perk him up and give him a bit more strength to carry on. Sadly this was never to be, as he'd died twenty minutes before we reached his home. Beside him had been the four most important people in his life: Val, Jamie, Kelly and Karen – a lifelong friend of Kelly's who Lenny thought of as another daughter. As he often said, they were his life. Everything he ever did, aimed for or achieved was for them, and how they felt about losing this rock-like husband, father and father-figure, I couldn't even begin to imagine, though knowing how I felt myself their pain must have been unbearable.

We all sat downstairs, either in the conservatory or garden – totally stunned. I'll never forget Val putting her arm on mine and asking me if I was alright. She'd just lost her husband an hour before, yet took time to worry about how I felt, which took strength like Lenny's, but of a different kind.

Shirley went up to see Lenny and say her last goodbyes. I know she told him how well the signing went, but what else she said remains private between her and Len. As for myself, though I have no fear of death, I just couldn't bring myself to look at the shell of my friend and of the man who had probably been the greatest influence of my life. How would our lives be now that he was gone out of it?

Leaving the family to grieve in private we set off home, facing the prospect of a miserable three-hour journey. Yet it didn't turn out like that. We drove in silence for perhaps half an hour, both lost in our thoughts, then simultaneously we said, 'Do you remember?' which set us off on a nostalgic trip down the years we'd known Lenny. We laughed and cried, and I thought then that though we would never see him in the flesh again, he'd always be with us. And two years down the line this has been proven – daily.

The following day the telephone rang constantly as

the media chased comments and quotes. Every news station carried the story that the Guv'nor had lost his toughest fight. Yet instead of finding this attention intrusive at such a time, we dealt with every call knowing that Lenny, showman that he was, would have loved every minute of the nationwide attention.

Twenty-four hours after Len had passed away, almost to the minute; we had a call from the publisher telling us that our book had jumped from nowhere straight into the coveted number one slot. My emotions were too mixed up to describe. I walked to the top of our field, looked up into the vast expanse of sky that Lincolnshire is famous for, and with tears streaming down my face said, 'You did it, Lenny. You beat them all.' Number one. Every author's dream. Never mind talk of 'for art's sake or self-fulfilment', bottom line says you've made it to the top and beaten off all the competition. Yet without Len to share the moment we'd worked together towards for so many years, any celebration was full of conflicting emotions. On one hand it was the greatest tribute imaginable for the big fella himself, but on the other hand I can say with all honesty that I would swap the success and plaudits that have followed, if it could mean that he was still with us.

The funeral that took place a week later was a display of respect not seen in the East End since that of Ronnie Kray's send off. Val, a very private person, who while supporting Len in every way kept in the background, would have preferred a simple family ceremony. But knowing her husband better than anyone else, she knew he would have liked his final journey to be like his life –

up front and in the public eye. At the same time it would allow those thousands of fans, for want of a better word, to pay their respects.

Friends and family gathered at the house on that glorious sunny August day, and Val, as strong as ever, had a word for everyone. She seemed to have put aside her own personal grief so that everything could run smoothly for her Lenny. The imaginative shapes of the floral tributes that arrived every minute seemed to have no boundary and soon the front garden was a blaze of colour – each associated in some way to the man himself. A boxing glove, a giant cup of tea, a cream cake – even a favourite dog painstakingly created from thousands of dried flowers.

Lenny was already in the chapel of rest at English's Funeral Parlour in Hoxton, and the schedule was that we would all drive there, then follow his horse-drawn carriage to the crematorium. At eleven o'clock an incredible convoy swept out of Bexleyheath and headed for the East End. Fifteen gleaming limousines followed by in excess of seventy other vehicles. At a third of a mile long it was an impressive sight. As we approached London small groups of people gave way to larger and larger crowds, until as we drew into Hoxton High Street the gathering filled the pavements from kerb to shopfront. That area of London was brought to a complete standstill as we queued in line while waiting for Lenny's coffin to be placed on the carriage up ahead, and the hundreds of wreaths were placed on and in cars up and down the line.

It was a very hot day so after ten minutes or so mourners began to get out of the cars to stand talking in huddled groups. Conveniently our car had stopped right outside a pub so we slipped inside and drank to Lenny's memory. An old man sitting in a corner beckoned me over and said, 'You know what? Years ago Lenny McLean was always in here 'cos it was what they called a singing pub then, with all the old songs and all that, and he loved it.' If you care to think that way we must have been guided into the place by the big fella – either that or fantastic coincidence.

Then we were off on a pre-planned route towards the City of London Crematorium at Manor Park. Four black head-tossing horses, drawing a carriage covered in floral messages from Val, Jamie and Kelly and in its wake the limousines equally covered. My family's tribute to Lenny was – and what else could it have been – a book. And we were proud to see that with no direction or specific request it was placed upright on the roof of the leading vehicle. As we drove through the packed streets a centre ribbon, stating simply 'Number One', broke free at one end and fluttered high in the air, and we focused on it. A tiny incident, but something that has stayed with me.

Looking out of the window I saw for the first time gigantic billboards displaying the poster for *Lock, Stock & Two Smoking Barrels*, as yet unreleased, which struck me as sadly ironic. Something else that would have made Lenny chuckle was that at every junction his coffin was given a salute by uniformed policemen directing the traffic.

When the cortege pulled into the Crematorium it

Above: **Lenny's funeral was a display of respect not seen in the East End since Ronnie Kray's send off. It would have given him a chuckle that at every junction his coffin was given a salute by uniformed policeman directing the traffic.**

had to pick its way through crowds of celebrities and past associates – many of them well-known faces. I won't name names in case I offend those I leave out, but one man's simple show of respect caught my eye and touched me. To one side, away from the crowd, Prince Naseem Hamed stood alone with his head bowed as Lenny's coffin drew past.

The service for family and friends was short, but said everything about why we were all there. John Huntley, a very dear friend of Len and his family, stood up and gave a moving personal eulogy that brought a few tears all round – though better still brought smiles as he repeated some phrases of Len's that we all knew so well. I admire John so much for what he did, knowing that it took a great effort just to stand up in front of all these people while in an emotional state himself.

Beside me sat a man who was not only a friend of Len's but also someone that often worked for him when necessary. A big man and, with respect, one whose tough appearance would make you think twice about getting on the wrong side of him. As the coffin began to move at the end of the service, an enormous hand gripped my shoulder in an unspoken show of compassion, which made me think that no one should be judged by the way they look.

As the curtains closed and Lenny was gone forever, I realised they'd also closed over a long and unforgettable chapter of my life.

That night as I lay in bed looking up at the sky one star stood out, brighter and larger than all the rest, and I said, 'Well, you got there Lenny.' Crazy? Over-fertile imagination? So what – the thought was a great comfort, as it had been when a similar happening had taken place after the death of my father. My mind wandered over what had been an emotional day then farther back as I relived incidents of the past years stretching right back to the first night we met. I remembered that first meeting with Lenny as though it were the previous day.

As I said in my foreword to *The Guv'nor* Reggie Kray

suggested I should call in on Len as well as a long list of other celebrities. Len was to be last on this list. After three days of touring around Southern England my mate Steve Pearce, who'd volunteered as chauffeur, and myself turned up in the East End at about six o'clock in the evening. Bearing in mind that I only knew this man by reputation who was, in his own words, an 'effing raving lunatic', the prospect of knocking on his door was, to say the least, a bit daunting.

After a bag of chips and a spruce up we arrived at 13 Strahan Road and were invited into the hall by Mrs McLean – Val. Then came that gruff voice that was to become so familiar. 'Go into the front room boys – with you in a minute.' Looking up, there was the man himself at the top of the stairs, dressed only in white underpants. If you think Lenny was huge on film, in the flesh he was a giant.

As Steve and I perched nervously on the edge of our seats in the lounge we just looked at each other, both unspeaking, wondering what we'd let ourselves in for. Val brought in the first of what would be thousands of cups of tea over the years – then disappeared into the kitchen. She was the cornerstone of the family yet preferred to keep in the background where business was concerned. God knows why but we were whispering like two schoolboys outside the headmaster's room – in anticipation.

As was to prove the norm in years to come, Lenny

Opposite: **If you thought Lenny was huge on film, in the flesh he was a giant!**

heralded his arrival long before reaching the door: a snatch of a song, a John Wayne drawl – 'Good evening my friends,' and there he was filling the doorway, grinning all over his face. After a crushing handshake from the biggest hands I have ever seen, Len wedged himself into a leather armchair, rolled a fag and, though I wasn't aware of it at the time, that was the point when we began a relationship that would change my life.

The reason for this meeting was to get Lenny's thoughts and opinions on Reggie and Ronnie Kray for a project instigated by Reggie. For three-quarters of an hour Len swung into interview mode as he spoke highly, if a bit formally, of the twins as he knew them. Once that was out of the way he visibly relaxed. When I got to know him better I understood why he was so serious on that initial interview. I was a stranger and apparently a journalist, asking him to comment on two underworld legends for whom he had the greatest respect. He wanted to do it right for my sake, theirs and his own. That was Lenny – ask anything from him and you got 110%.

Business, as he saw it, out of the way, he shouted, 'Val babe, you got a minute?' Through she came and he said to her, 'Sweetheart, this writer fella just asked me if your kettle was broke.' Even as my neck reddened up I could see Val was quite used to Len's wind-up as she went off to make more tea. As we drank it we were entertained by the vanishing coin trick. This man's hands were like shovels, yet Paul Daniels couldn't have improved on the act as he plucked fifty pence coins from our ears, collars or pockets.

Suddenly he said, 'They're making a film about me

you know.' Little did I know that that film would haunt us both for years to come, and I'm convinced ultimately the stress would contribute to his death. But right then I was impressed, as I was expected to be. Out came the script, while he gave me all the details on the casting and finances, and that it was to be made at Pinewood Studios. OK, I was naïve then, but no more than Len who at that time believed if Pinewood was on the letterhead everything had to be kosher.

So when he said, 'You're a writer, you're on the firm [referring to Reg Kray], what about me putting your name down to write the book of the film?' Whoa, hang on, I thought. I'm getting out of my depth here. Yes I was a writer but I knew my limitations, and rubbing shoulders with executive producers at this famous studio was well outside anything I thought I could aspire to. I could well imagine the suits at Pinewood with their twenty million budgets saying, 'Who the fuck is this bloke masquerading as a scriptwriter?'

I said to Len, 'Thanks for your confidence in me and for the offer, but I'm not high-profile enough to take on something like this.' His reply was lesson one in what was to become years of his kind-hearted pursuit to educate and push me forward in life.

He gave me that look of his – jaw pulled in, eyebrows furrowed. 'Son,' he said, 'never think you ain't good enough to do anything you want. It's all up here,' and he tapped his forehead. 'I never went into a fight thinking I was going to get beat, and I never was. Nothing to do with being flash. Believe in yourself and always aim high and

one day you'll be up there with the best of them. Are you in?' What could I say but 'Yes'? 'Good boy. Now whatever deal we get it's down the middle for both of us. Give us your hand.' And that was that. We were to have many business ups and downs in the years to come, but Lenny never again mentioned percentages or who was to get what. His handshake was a firm contract – stronger than anything on paper.

'Val! These chaps said can they have a drink of water?' The tea arrived and Lenny launched into a non-stop monologue of anecdotes from his life. His Mum and Dad, the hated stepfather Jim Irwin, borstal, fighting, Mafia, and an endless stream of stories – punctuated by tea and roll-ups.

I was just thinking to myself that this man is like everyone's favourite uncle, when he reached the point of talking about his time in prison. As he recalled how a young kid called Mark Thornborrow was being apparently tormented by the screws who had just brought him back from court after being given a life sentence for murder, he physically relived the moment. As he described watching the boy's treatment through a glass partition, he went in a second from amiable uncle to awe-inspiring monster. Jumping up he smashed on imaginary glass screaming, 'You c—s – let that little baby through.' He seemed to have doubled in size; veins stood out in his neck, the muscles in his arms and shoulders strained against his shirt and sweat beaded his forehead. No words

Opposite: 'Son,' Lenny said, 'never think you ain't good enough to do anything you want. I never went into a fight thinking I was going to get beat, and I never was.

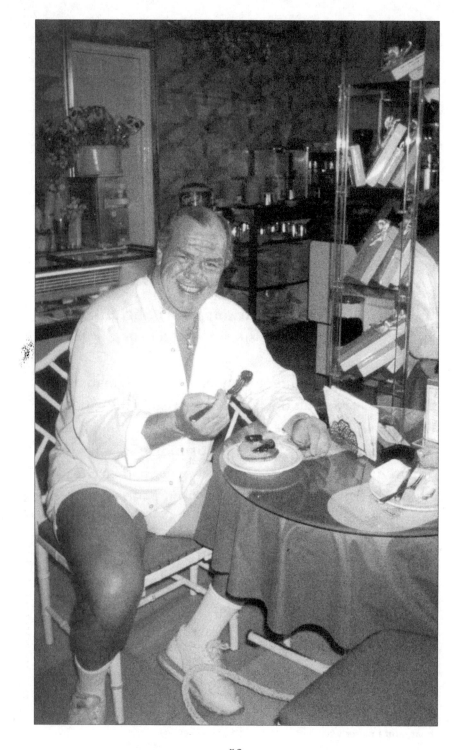

or image on film could have brought home to me the frightening power of this man they called the Guv'nor.

Story over, he settled comfortably back in his armchair as though nothing had happened, oblivious to the fact that he'd shown a side to himself usually kept outside the house. More tea, more fags and it was time to leave but not before spotting the camera I always carried. He said, 'Do you want a couple of snaps?' He wasn't full of his own importance, or up his own arse like too many celebrities; he knew that everyone liked to be photographed with the big fella, and showman that he was he was giving us our money's worth.

Steve sprang into classic 'photo with boxer' pose – playful punch to the chin. I raised my eyes to the ceiling and instead he put his arm round Lenny, falling a bit short of actually being able to reach round that massive frame. This photo hangs proudly in Steve's hallway – all these years later he is still honoured to have known the legend.

I remember talking to a film producer who was old enough to have worked with Hollywood stars in the days when they really lived up to the term. He told me that Lenny had charisma and presence equal to that of such names as Burt Lancaster, Kirk Douglas or Charlton Heston. We're not talking acting abilities here, but sheer personality. He said that if any of these names were in a room they filled it without saying a word or moving a muscle. I saw a great example of this with Lenny when we went to a press launch of a TV series he was in. After the

Opposite: **If there was one thing Lenny enjoyed more than a good fight, it was a nice cream cake!**

screening a press get together was held in the conference area. Unintentionally Len stole the show from the other actors who were household names. Remember he was a new boy to the game, a novice. Yet without exception he was surrounded by reporters and TV cameras. Looking round the room I could see a number of long faces and one or two angry ones – a bit upset by this minor role player in the series getting all the attention. They couldn't blame Len; he just stood there while the media flocked around him.

That first evening at Len's place we wrapped it up about 11.00 p.m. I assured Len that yes I would get straight on with sorting out the book business – we got a crushing hug each and set off home with head spinning. Though he knew my journey was three hours, he was on the phone after an hour and a half making sure through my wife that I would be on the phone to Pinewood first thing. Typical Len! Back home I tried to convey to Shirley the dynamic character I'd spent the evening with, but gave up. Words were not enough – she'd have to find out for herself.

First thing next morning I got in touch with the film company to find that earlier still Len had been on to them saying he wanted me on board. I couldn't believe it. I'd known him for a matter of five hours and already he was rooting for me. Eventually I'd accept that this was normal for Len. If he said he'd do something, it was done, and done there and then. No excuses, no reminders. Unlike the straight business world where a cheque can be 'in the post' for weeks, and calls go unanswered.

As far as Lenny was concerned the cameras were ready to roll, but talking to the producer I got the impression, through hesitancy on his part, that things were not as far advanced as suggested. Yes, he was quite willing for me to take on the film/book, but he told me not to do anything for the moment. Wait for this – wait for that. I never said what I thought to Lenny, but instead put to him that perhaps an autobiography might be something to do in tandem. Instead of jumping at the idea he said, 'I dunno. I had some mug try that a year or so back and I had to fuck him off when I read what he'd done.' I knew nothing about this but confident that his story had to be told to a wider audience I talked him round by assuring him we'd work closely together. One minute reluctant, five minutes later enthusiastic. 'Go on then son, get something fixed up. Lively!'

Within a week we had the offer of a contract from one of the larger publishing houses in the country, and a meeting arranged in their prestigious offices with lunch to follow. Strange really, here was a man who rubbed shoulders with the most notorious of gangsters, fought and beat the hardest of opponents, told the Mafia to stick their offers up their arse – yet he was nervous of this meeting. Perhaps he felt slightly out of his depth approaching this world of intellectuals and 'stuffy suits' and wasn't sure how he would come across. To him the film game was a piece of piss, full of people who'd smooth-talk the shirt off your back – people he understood. The publishing world was an unknown quantity.

As it turned out, for all Lenny's 'How do I look? How shall I handle it?' on the way to the meeting, after ten minutes he had everyone at his feet. Allowing that my initial approach to the publishers hardly gave a clue to the real Lenny, I think they were rather expecting some grunting thug to turn up. Had anyone like him ever walked through those doors? I doubt it.

For the first few minutes he was overly polite and talked with a slight plum in his mouth. That wasn't him and he couldn't sustain it without dropping into his normal mode of storyteller and comedian. The men stared at him in awe, the ladies loved him. If at any time the general focus was directed elsewhere, Len took the opportunity to whisper to my wife, 'How'm I doing?' What could she say? He was doing what he was best at – being the funny and highly entertaining star of the show, and we were proud to be associated with him. At the lunch that followed he not only kept our table laughing and waiting for the next story, but every other table in this posh restaurant. When we first sat down I could hear conversations all around the room drying up as everyone looked in amazement at this genial giant. And when he, as he often did for effect, came out in a loud voice with 'Course, that fucking murder charge didn't do me no favours,' you could have heard a pin drop.

The director of the company at the time was a man who, I say with the greatest respect, was the epitome of everyone's idea of a publisher. Elderly, grey-suited and very respectable. As he had to leave us before the lunch he offered his hand to Len. Lenny looked at him and said, 'You're alright, come 'ere and give us a hug.' With that he lifted the man clean off his feet in a bear-like cuddle. All we could see were those two eyes peering over Lenny's broad shoulders. By the look on his face once he was back on the floor, it was obvious he was a bit taken aback, but I would think he's dined out on that story many times since.

A week later we sat down together in Len's front room and I began to take down his story. One of the things I loved about him was that once he trusted you, and you got that quickly or not at all, nothing was held back – and I mean nothing. He told me things, though not for publication, that if I passed them on could have got him or others prison time. Although he invariably added, 'Just between you and me', he never felt the need to threaten dire consequences if I opened my mouth.

A couple of years later the two of us were at a showbiz celebrity function in London when Lenny said to me, 'See that geezer over there in the black suit?' I looked in the direction of his nod, to see an actor who had been at the height of his fame back in the seventies and someone who, like most other people, I thought was one of the best.

I said to Len, 'Yeah, that's whatsisname, shall we go over and shake his hand?'

'Shake his hand? I should go over there and shake his fucking neck.' Seeing the surprised look on my face he added, 'Remember that story I told you about that doctor in the nick whose young relative was being rumped by a famous actor? Well that's the dirty bastard over there. He's already had some over all that business, but it weren't enough 'cos he's still walking.'

I was stunned that this top man, who incidentally is still on the screen, was a perverted child molester, but more so by the fact that Len had entrusted me with knowledge that would have been worth fifty thousand for a phone call to any one of the Sunday tabloids. You can't buy trust like that and I personally don't sell it.

Another time as we sat in his conservatory early one morning he said to me, 'Drink that tea up lively, I want you to give me a hand with a bit of work.' On the way we picked up another man and Len introduced me as 'My book man and he's safe.' As he drove towards the city they explained that access was needed to the office of a 'businessman' and I was to be the way in, on the pretext of an interview with this person. We were welcomed in and as I questioned the man on various matters, out of the corner of my eye I could see Len's friend discreetly planting a bug under the desk. At a casual nod I wound up the interview and we left the office. Len and myself slipped into a coffee bar a couple of doors up, while the other fella stood in a nearby shop doorway with a transmitter to his ear. If things went to plan a throwaway line that had been fed to the man in the office should result in a hurried phone call. And if he was as dodgy as the other two suspected, the incriminating conversation would be picked up and acted upon.

A thumbs-up to us through the coffee bar window meant a result. Now we had to reverse the process and retrieve the bug. Full of apologies for taking up his time we re-entered the office to collect the notebook I had deliberately left behind. We chatted just long enough for the bug to be removed then we were away – job done to everyone's satisfaction. What all this James Bond stuff led to I've no idea and knew enough not to ask questions. But back at Lenny's home the first thing the other fella did was to shrug off his overcoat saying, 'I'll be glad to get this bastard off. I'm sweating cobs.' Underneath he was wearing a bullet-proof vest and the ominous bulge at his waist band made me think I was as far away from the Lincolnshire Wolds as it was possible to get and into another world that ordinary people never get a glimpse of.

Lenny's only reference to what had gone down was a touch to the side of his nose and a 'Good boy'.

This trust and unreserved honesty made his reaction over my answer to one of his casual questions quite explosive and it still makes me laugh to remember it. While working around London I always stayed with my sister and brother-in-law. Len knew this and during one of our breaks where we just chatted about nothing in particular, he asked me what my sister did. 'She's an Estate Agent, Len.'

'Oh yeah, and what about her old man?'

No point in keeping secrets so I told him. 'Police. Chief Inspector.'

He sat bolt upright. 'Fuck me, no!' he said. Then calling through to the kitchen he shouted, ''Ere Val, you ain't gonna believe this – Peter's brother-in-law's top old bill.' For the rest of the afternoon he kept shaking his head and saying, 'I'm waiting for you to tell me this is a wind-up.'

Some time after my relative was to leap in Len's estimation of coppers in general. A millionaire business friend of his was driving through South London when he was hemmed in by two unmarked police cars and dragged out of his Mercedes. In the struggle that followed this friend put down one policeman and threw another over the bonnet of his car. Overpowered and handcuffed he was forced into the back of the police vehicle where it was discovered this arrest and the brawl that followed was all down to mistaken identity. Apologies all round? No chance. He was charged with assault. Released on bail he was straight on to Lenny who, if he couldn't fix problems, invariably knew somebody who could. Len came off the phone and said, 'Peter, we've all got to graft together on this. Have a word with your brother-in-law and see what he can do. This friend of mine is a straightgoer but he's one of us and I won't see him rumped.'

That evening I explained to my in-law what had happened. He told me that unfortunately there was nothing he could do. 'Before my time, perhaps twenty-five years ago, a word in the right ear could make a lot of difference, but it doesn't happen anymore. So all I can do is give your friend a bit of advice.' He did, and I passed it on. So what with this, plus a good brief, Lenny's pal had his problem squared away by the following evening. My brother-in-law hadn't been able to intervene in the process of law, but as far as Lenny was concerned he had shown an interest and that was more than enough to make him alright in his eyes.

Too many people of importance or celebrity status jealously guard their position. They don't want you to know too much, talk to their contacts or give any information that might help to make you equal to them. Most are friendly enough on the surface, but there is always a point when a barrier comes down. Not with Lenny. What he knew, you knew. His friends were your friends.

During the time we spent sitting in that front room the telephone interrupted us endlessly. Though disconcerted at first, I soon got used to the fact that at the end of his conversation he would say to whoever was calling, ''Ere, have a word with my book man.' The phone would be thrust into my hand and I'd find myself talking to complete strangers – celebrities, top people, faces, some as far away as America.

If sitting indoors with Lenny listening to his endless stories was an experience, going out with him was something else. In the East End he was the local hero and we couldn't walk ten yards without someone wanting to shake his hand. This was carried on to a lesser degree in the city, but again we couldn't go far without taxis slowing down for the driver to shout a greeting. As tough and menacing as Lenny could look, such was that charisma I mentioned that he could get away with liberties that few other men could. Any pretty young lady he spotted walking towards us would be accosted with, 'Ah, ain't you beautiful – give us a smile,' and ten out of ten he got a hello, a smile and a giggle – no offence taken.

Above: **In the East End Lenny was the local hero and we couldn't walk ten yards without someone wanting to shake his hand. He is pictured here with Charlie Kray.**

Same with children and the old, he gave them both affection and respect. Two examples spring to mind. One was when he met my mother-in-law at King's Cross, a lady who was brought up at The Angel in Islington and well into her seventies. They had a bit of cockney banter between them then he said to her, 'I love all you old people, come 'ere, Floss, an' give's a cuddle.' With which he lifted her off her feet and gave her a twirl. Before he left he said to her, 'Listen, if you or any of your mates ever get any agg' from tearaways or anybody, let me know and they'll never do it again.'

The other occasion was when he visited our home in Boston. Our son Peter, quite young at the time, came in from school and Lenny stood up and shook his hand with a respect not normally given to children. They chatted comfortably for a while, then Len said, 'You know what young Peter? When they start making my film, I'm going to take you to Pinewood and show you all round the James Bond set. But you'll have to bring one of your pals, 'cos otherwise none of your mates at school would believe you spent the day with the Guv'nor.' Years later our son still remembers how Lenny had to squeeze himself into one of our large armchairs and the fact that his own hand was swallowed up in Lenny's massive handshake. The promised outing, like the film, never happened. But towards the end he said, 'I never did take your boy down the studios, did I? Make sure you tell him that I haven't forgot and when I've shook off this illness and we get the film going, I'll have him down there double quick.'

As big and as tough as he might have been, away from work he didn't give off a single threatening vibe. Which is a contrast to when his book man was shown disrespect in an East End gym. As was shown at the end of his life, Lenny's answer to feeling under the weather was a strenuous workout. He had a cold that would've put ordinary men into bed for a week. We went to the gym and I watched as he spent a full hour bench pressing weights, one-arm press-ups and running on the machine. When he was done he took me over to the refreshment bar, called to the barman and said, 'This is my book man. He wants to talk to you about what I do here, so give him a cup of tea and be nice because this fella's going to make me a lot of money.' Then he took off for the showers.

The man behind the bar gave me the tea as instructed, then politely said, 'I've got a bit of business at the other end of the bar. Give me five minutes and we'll have a chat.' No problem – to me anyway.

I was just checking the batteries on my tape recorder when the doors smashed back on their hinges and Lenny ran past my table screaming at the top of his lungs and made towards the barman who was talking to a thick-set fella further down the gym. At first I thought Len was larking about then realised he was deadly serious. I flicked on the recorder and watched open-mouthed at a display of aggression I'd never witnessed before or since. This was a Lenny I didn't know. He grabbed hold of the barman, who was no lightweight, and flung him away from the other man, shouting, 'No respect – You ain't got no fucking respect.' Then, grabbing the other man by the throat, he almost lifted him off the floor, all the while keeping up this torrent of abuse. 'Get out of here you dirty grassing c—t. What are you? What are you? What are you? You're a filthy grass – a no value c—t.' Eventually the bloke broke away and ran for the door and whatever had gone down was over.

I didn't realise until Len explained why the ruck had happened and that the bloke had me to thank for not getting beaten senseless. I felt a bit guilty when Lenny made the barman apologise to me because he had told me he'd be gone for five minutes, but where he'd compounded the offence was to ignore me in favour of talking to this guy – a man, as told in the book, marked down as a grass. Afterwards, Len told me that if I hadn't been there he would've torn his face off.

That tape recording has a surreal quality about it. Len's booming voice, the grass's grunts, the higher-pitched barman's voice pleading, 'Please stop Len, you're ruining my business.' The whole thing against a background of pop music. All because of respect – or lack of it.

I'd never seen Lenny fight live. He'd given that up some time before I met him, so as far as I was concerned it was hard to reconcile what I'd seen on film and heard so much about, with the placid and humorous bear of a man that I'd come to know. That incident, although a one-off, opened my eyes to the sheer power and ferocity that had made him what he was – the Guv'nor.

When we first began to put together the material for his book, Lenny came over in conversations as an angry man. He'd not long finished a prison term with a murder charge hanging over his head. The mental stress, plus the drugs that had been used on him, left him, as he put it, 'completely fucked up in the head'. On top of this, because of the very nature of his reputation, he thought that his book should reflect the raving lunatic he liked to portray. But that was really just a public front, for I've never met anyone who was less raving or lunatic than him. I knew there was more to this man than he liked to let people see, so I encouraged him to talk about his childhood – his mother, and anything away from the violence he dealt in. At first he gave me the old 'cross-eye' saying, 'Leave it out Peter, this stuff's fucking boring,

Above: As time went on Lenny put his anger behind him. Much of the reason for this was to do with the calming influence of Val. He was tired of dealing with scum and low lifes.

innit?' But it was more a question than a statement, and after a while he slipped quite easily into what he might have thought of as softer aspects of his character, which – as a quarter of a million readers would agree – became the heart of his story.

As time went on he seemed to put that anger behind him and move on. Much of the reason for this was to do with the calming influence of Val. I don't recall a specific point where he made a conscious decision to move away from the working life he'd had up until then. What I do know is that he often spoke of how tired he was of dealing with scum and low lifes, though when he was speaking like this he wasn't referring to people he worked with or of underworld figures, many of whom he had the greatest respect for. He meant those at the lower end of his world. A constant stream of drunks, druggies, bullies and loud-mouthed plastic gangsters who he had to bash up or straighten out every day of his working life. What he wanted was to leave all that behind and move into areas where he could earn a living amongst proper people.

'Proper people' to Lenny were film directors, writers, actors and producers who he could see made a decent living in a respectable world. A world that never had to get involved with the seamier sides of life, and where those within it were not constantly looking over their shoulders. The way into this was going to be his book and his film, but there were problems with both that drove him crazy with frustration.

The film, which had been on the drawing board years before I ever met Len, was mired down in promises and false starts. Endlessly going into pre-production – next week, next month, early next year – those involved moving the goalposts every time it seemed as though something tangible was about to happen. As backers, Lenny and friends had sunk a considerable amount of money into the production company, but it was never enough and more requests were made on him for more cash, without one single frame being shot. It was going nowhere.

Neither was the book, for somewhere along the line it had got tied into the film and one wasn't going to happen without the other. Understandably, for maximum publicity the publisher at that time wanted to coincide their publication with the screenplay hitting the silver screen. And as frustrating as it was to us they just wouldn't budge,

Below: Lenny had a word for everyone – and everyone had time for the Guv'nor.

no matter how many times Lenny asked them to bring the book out on its own. Their answer was always the same. 'We understand from the producers that pre-production is imminent, so we think it's best to wait.' Stalemate!

Then a combination of events, none to do with Lenny or myself, resulted in our contract being cancelled overnight and we were back to square one.

Before this happened though, we were invited to the prestigious launch of the publisher's new offices. With terrorist problems rife in London at that time, entry was strictly restricted to those wearing security tags. So by the time we joined the queue it snaked up three flights of stairs. Now Lenny had a short attention span when it came to standing around doing nothing, so after five minutes he had the fidgets. He looked up the stairs – he looked down the stairs. He hummed a short snatch of a song, straightened his tie, whispered 'Fuck this' in my ear half a dozen times, and in all didn't know what to do next to combat this inactivity.

Directly in front of us, and up a couple of steps, stood an attractively petite woman with long dark hair. I saw Lenny study the back of her head a couple of times and just knew he was going to do something. After a bit of thought he put his hand in his pocket, drew out a fifty pence piece, then tapped on the woman's shoulder saying, 'Excuse me tiny bum – you seen this?' As she turned he went into his disappearing coin trick. I recognised this lady immediately but I know Lenny didn't. Trick over, she smiled, thanked him and turned to face up the stairs again.

Two minutes of boredom passed until he tapped her on the shoulder once more. "Ere short stuff, do you work for this mob or 'ave you done a book or what?'

She turned again and said, 'Indirectly I work for this mob. I'm Lynda La Plante, and yes I've done a book.'

Lenny went, 'Nah, you ain't – are you?'

She said, 'Yes, and you're Lenny McLean – I've heard all about you.'

That pleased him, but he said, 'If that's who you are, my mate here [pointing at me] wants to smack your bum, 'cos you nicked our title for that TV series of yours.' [*The Governor*].

I raised my arms as much as to say 'would I dare?' but she laughed saying, 'Sorry about that Lenny, but I don't think there could be any confusion between the two stories.' Mollified by her remarks, Len was won over and they ended up chatting like old friends for the rest of our wait in the queue, and half an hour or so in the reception room. Lenny might not have recognised her, but he was well aware of her reputation as one of the country's top writers.

From that night right up until his death he often referred to letting Lynda see his finished book: 'Just to see what she thinks of it.' On eventual publication he asked me to make sure she got a copy, which I did. Then, by return, came a personal letter to him praising a wonderful read and inviting him to lunch as soon as she returned from her summer retreat abroad. Sadly he passed away before the pre-arranged date, but that letter meant a great deal to Len. He read and re-read it and talked about or showed it to everyone. A small gesture from her but to a man who'd walked a long and dangerous path down the years, here was a proper person with fame and stature in the literary world telling him that his efforts should be a bestseller. It meant he'd achieved what he'd set out to do and was on his way.

That same evening Lenny, myself and a friend of his were hemmed in the centre of a large group of 'bookish' people. Now I'd be the first to admit that in appearance author is not the first impression that springs to mind when first meeting me, and doubly so for Len and his mate. For a start each of us stood head and shoulders above the rest and due to the noise and crush of heaving bodies, we were forced into talking in whispered tones with our heads almost touching. Suddenly the smallest woman in the room squirreled herself between the three of us, her head popping up from nowhere a foot below our chins, saying 'Who are you three? You look like you're planning a bank robbery.'

Lenny leant down, put his arm around her and said, 'No, we ain't working tonight sweetheart. I was just telling these two fellas 'ere that you was the beautifullest woman in the place.' The McLean charm or what? He made a fan for life that night.

Although Len was well pissed off with what had happened with film and book, he never allowed himself to be despondent for long – it wasn't in his nature. Move on – You've got to keep moving on. As one door closes (or two in this case) another opens, and this happened when he met Paul Knight, the highly-thought-of director of *London's Burning*. Paul was currently putting together a new TV series based on Customs and Excise, to be called *The Knock*, a term used by the same group when they go after the villains in the final round-up. With no acting experience, save for a series of TV adverts years previously, Len put himself up for the part of what else but a tough guy. Paul Knight, metaphorically knocked out by Len's size and personality, and no doubt swayed by his authentic background, immediately gave Len the job. But not before arguing for weeks with others in casting, who felt this 'real life baddy' might be more hindrance than help. To his credit, and Len's eternal gratitude, Paul stuck to his guns and wouldn't consider anyone else.

This was to be his first step on the ladder towards a career in the acting game and Len never forgot or failed to credit this one man for making it possible.

Lenny was neither a villain in the true sense, or a gangster, which as the name suggests is being part of a gang. 'If you can't do a bit of work on your own, or you have to be ten-handed in a fight, you're nothing,' Len used to say. But in the perception of those who didn't know him he was both these things, and it pushed the ratings and the publicity for the series way up in the charts, making it an enormous hit. The media coverage – mainly articles on Leonard McLean, the 'real thing' – boosted its popularity beyond what it might have achieved without him.

Now Lenny's contract was just for the first series of six weeks. At the end of the run he was to be arrested and sent to prison for many years. End of Eddie Davis, end of

Len's first acting job. But Paul Knight didn't want to lose this wonderful asset to his programme so he got his scriptwriters to rework the script giving Eddie a suspended sentence and by doing so allowed Len to return and boost the viewing figures all over again.

I remember going on set with him in the second series when he had an involved storyline opposite Dennis Waterman. As always he put every ounce of effort into learning his lines and making sure that if anyone spoiled a take it wasn't going to be him, no matter how new he was at the game. The two of us and another rookie actor by the name of Tony McMahon ended up in the green room. For a while we sat around drinking tea and having a laugh about nothing in particular until the pair of them began bouncing their lines off of me. I had Lenny saying to me (I was taking on Dennis Waterman's character) 'I'm Eddie Davis, and nobody gives me the run-around. Was that menacing enough Peter? Hang on, I'll try it another way. I'm Eddie Davis and I don't – oh, bollocks, what was that again? Never mind – this'll get 'em. I'm Eddie Davis so get on your horse and drink your milk.'

I said, 'That's John Wayne.'

'I know. Fucking good innit?' and he burst out laughing.

Young Tony, the other actor, had one line to say – his first in front of a camera – and it was, 'What's it got to do with us John?' I wouldn't have believed one sentence could be repeated two hundred times and each be different from the one before. He paced up and down saying it to me, to Len, the wall and everything else in the

room. Still, his scene wasn't until the following day so he was all right for another two hundred variations. Len's was in half an hour.

We went down on set, which was a mock-up of a pub, and as they were setting the scene up Lenny said to me,

'Go on son, get yourself up to that bar.'

'What?'

'Sit up at the bar and you'll be on the telly with me and Dennis.'

'Len, I haven't got an equity card, I'll be thrown out.'

'Fuck 'em. Gimme a shout if anybody puts the collar on you.'

Next thing it was taken out of my hands as the director ushered me and other professional actors up to the bar. It just so happened I was placed face on to camera so that I would be picked up (if only for five seconds) between Len and Dennis in the shot. Tony was positioned facing me, back to camera. As we waited he whispered without moving his lips, 'Change places.'

'Nope.'

'Go on, swap round.'

'Nope.'

He should have been a ventriloquist. 'Don't be a c—t, I need to be seen, I'm gonna be an actor.'

'Tough, I might want to be an actor myself after this.' His heartbreaking pleas fell on deaf ears, but it was only a joke between us. Whether it's standard practise or not I couldn't say, but the pint glass stuck in front of me was

Opposite: Lenny on the set of *Lock, Stock & Two Smoking Barrels* with Laura Baily, one-time girlfriend of Richard Gere.

real lager. Like Lenny I'm not a drinker, so why I didn't just take a small sip I'll never know. But putting myself into the role of drinker at the bar, I half emptied the glass. Eleven takes later I couldn't stop my eyes crossing and the next few hours passed in a pleasant sort of daze. End of the day my pay-off was a treasured video memory of myself on screen with the big fella, plus – and Lenny made sure I was squared up – a ninety pound cheque for an hour's work. Me taking over Tony's spot in front of the camera didn't do any harm at all for he would eventually go on to star in *Lock, Stock & Two Smoking Barrels* – all down to Lenny's guidance and influence. As with Tony and many, many others, myself included, if Len took to someone no effort on his part was too great to make on their behalf. He was comfortable and confident in himself and what he did and it took nothing away from him to help friends achieve dreams they might not have otherwise without his help.

Some time later he got a call from the producers of a film called *The Fifth Element*, which would star Bruce Willis. He went along for a screen test, but unusually was not told exactly what role he was up for. He did the business, passed with flying colours, and was offered the part. He said 'Yeah, that's OK but you haven't told me who I'm playing yet. I ain't gonna finish up acting the arse end of a donkey.' Considering the man he was, there

Opposite: Asked if he got nervous in front of the camera, he replied: 'My son, I've faced guns, knives and tough guys coming at me ten handed. I was beaten senseless as a little baby and sweated twelve months behind the door with a murder change over my head and I never knew what nerves were. So no, cameras don't worry me at all.'

was a bit of reluctance to spell it out, but eventually they told him that he would be portraying a chief of police. He told me later that his reaction was, 'Do fucking what? I can't do that; I've got a rep to think about.' When it was explained that the film was set in the year 2050 and his futuristic character would be nothing like present-day 'Old Bill' he accepted.

When shooting began, Lenny had this 'bright spark of a kid' run ragged fetching him soft drinks. 'Good boy – slip away and get me a nice glass of lemonade – lively.'

This went on for some days until someone said to Len, 'Do you know who that young fella is?'

I could imagine that furrowed brow. 'Nah. Who is he?'

'It's Lee Evans and he's a big star.'

Typical Len, his reaction was, 'Well fuck me, I thought he was the tea boy.'

We've all been there, fetching and carrying for Lenny, and I'm sure Lee didn't take any more exception than any of us did. He and Lenny hit it off, and from what Len told me, they had some great laughs during the rest of filming.

Another time there was a scene where Lenny had to kneel down and lean over the body of a dying soldier. With cameras rolling Len whispered in the ear of this apparently unconscious man, 'You had your helmet polished lately?' making the actor react with a hysterical fit of laughing, ruining the take. Len was asked to behave, but knowing him I'm sure it didn't alter his humorous outbursts.

I asked him if he ever got nervous in front of the

cameras – after all, even the best and most experienced admit to butterflies before a performance. Stupid question. 'My son,' he said 'I've faced guns, knives and tough guys coming at me ten handed. I was beaten senseless as a little baby and sweated twelve months behind the door with a murder charge over my head and I never knew what nerves was. Perhaps I haven't got none. So no, cameras don't worry me at all. This film business is like kids playing pretend games, 'cept they stuff your pockets full of cash for doing it, and I love every minute of it.' And he did. 'I've left all that other shit behind me now and I'm on the way up. I ain't big-headed; there's a long way to go and I've got a lot to learn but make me right, I'm willing to make the effort.'

In a throwback to his heroes of the screen when he was a small boy, Lenny always saw himself as comparable to an American actor by the name of Victor McLagen. Anyone over fifty will remember him well – any younger perhaps not at all. But Lenny was right; there were many similarities between the two. McLagen, a giant of a man with the features of one who'd had a fight or two, was the real thing. Invariably, whatever role he took on he was always himself, usually bursting out of a dress suit, his performance tough and overlaid with humour, same as Lenny.

No question, with the right parts, plus his single-minded perseverance, Len would have worked his way up to mirror the career of his hero. But sadly, even as he put every effort into portraying the psychotic Barry the Baptist in *Lock Stock*, the end of his promising career was already in sight. Ill and showing it, he put on his best performance so far. The film went on to become best of 1998, as by coincidence did his book. And down to this the future careers of all involved were guaranteed – except Lenny's. Though he played relatively in the background, his part was nevertheless carried out with a conviction that had great impact, reflected by the fact that originally those giant billboards advertising the film carried Len's profile in the position later occupied by a shotgun-wielding Vinnie Jones.

Life, as always, has carried on in the two years since his death, but his presence has stayed with me. Various photographs grin down from the walls in my home. His best autobiography award plus other memorabilia decorates the office and his features greet us in every bookstore in the land. But more tangibly, my follow-up book was with Mike Reid, a man who Lenny felt I should get in touch with. 'Mike's good stuff, and when I'm a bit stronger me an' you'll slip down to Elstree and I'll introduce you to him.' Lenny never recovered enough to carry this out, but his name was all the introduction needed and Mike and I shook hands on a deal, resulting in another chart success.

I never fail to acknowledge that much of what I have today is down to the unselfish concern and interest in my career of that one man. Which leaves me with one last memory.

It is of one of the last things Lenny ever said to me. We were talking in his conservatory shortly before his death, when he just looked at me and said, 'Peter, I ain't 'alf glad I met you.' I couldn't have asked for a higher compliment. So Lenny, all I can say now is I ain't 'alf glad I met you too. Thanks for everything. God bless pal. No one will ever replace you. The Guv'nor. My friend.

PETER GERRARD

CHAPTER 2

Lenny The Child

I've never been one for looking back –
I never saw the point. It didn't matter how
much I might have wanted to change my past,
it just couldn't be done, so I never really tried.
I was always looking forward, that was me – to
that deal round the corner or the clever move
round the next; on my toes all the time.

IF LENNY had never known anything else but the brutal treatment he suffered at the hands of his stepfather Jim Irwin, it would have been bad enough. But he had real and very fond memories of his own father and I can imagine that the contrast between the two must have been devastating for a child of his age.

As he nursed bruises and broken bones, or spent summer evenings shut in a darkened bedroom, his mind must have found escape in recalling those brief but happy years when he had a real man in the house.

He told me that he often talked to a photograph of his Dad, and for many years believed that one day he would walk through the door, throw Jim Irwin out and they'd all be happy again. It could never happen. As months turned into years of living under the tyranny of his stepfather he slowly came to terms with that fact and became hardened

Opposite: Lenny often used to talk to a photograph of his Dad, and for many years believed that one day he would walk through the door, throw his hated stepfather out, and they'd all be happy again.

to the kicks and punches. As with whatever he faced throughout his life he learned to accept that that's how his life was meant to be, though he could never accept this violence when it was directed at the rest of the family. In later years I'm sure this was the reason that he was so passionate about protecting the weak from bullies.

Not once in all the conversations we had about his ill treatment did he criticise his mother. He never questioned why she hadn't tried to protect him because he'd answered that for himself thirty-five years ago and accepted that she was as much a victim as he was.

As he said in his book, much of what he forced himself to remember from those early days brought a lump to his throat. And I know he found it a moving experience when we both went back to Godwin House in the East End, the scene of so many traumas for him. He told me this was the first time he'd set eyes on the place in over thirty years.

Opposite: Lenny never wanted to make any mileage out of his traumatic and painful childhood.

Above: Len never spoke of his mum with anything but the utmost respect. This happy photo was taken on his parents' wedding day, before the trauma of their later life.

Prior to this we'd spent weeks talking about what had gone on here, so the memories were all fresh in his mind and I could see it affected him. It was a strange experience for me as well. I'd mentally lived every moment with him and now here we were, and I was able to put flesh on the bones of what up until then for me had been fiction.

With a stretch of imagination I could see this scruffy

Top: A young Lenny with Bill Boy, outside Godwin House in the East End.

Below and opposite: Boy to man: it was the punches he suffered as a young lad from his stepfather that turned him into the awesome fighting machine he became, with an obsession for protecting people from bullies…

block, as it must have been all those years ago when the McLean family moved in, full of hope and excitement for the future. I like to think that Lenny deliberately parked the car in roughly the same spot where they would have all jumped down from that old lorry, but I didn't ask because I could sense he didn't want to talk. So we sat in silence looking round, both thinking our thoughts.

Over to the right was Morgan's shop where young Lenny used to buy his barely-flavoured cubes of ice – long disused and boarded up. Almost in front of us was the communal waste bin from where Lenny had quietly pulled out the go-kart to carry the badly beaten Kruger to his Nan's. In my mind I could see this man beside me as a child, hollering like an Indian as he rode an imaginary horse around the tarmac forecourt followed by Alfie and Timmy Hayes. I could see him swinging upside down on these rusting railings and with no effort at all I could see Barry, Kruger and Lenny sitting on these same low walls sucking lollies to death and talking about the fight with Brian Hyams.

Lenny never spoke, just sat there lost in thought – probably the same thoughts I was having – then he said, 'Let's go up and see if anybody's living in the flat.' As it turned out the place was empty, but it allowed us both, head to head, to peer through the letterbox, while Lenny gave a whispered guided tour. Our view was limited but to me it was like looking through a window into the past, and images of what had taken place here, good and bad, raced through my mind like a film. 'See that door? That's the one my uncle Jimmy smashed down to get at Irwin.

Above: Lenny pictured by his father's little pauper's grave

Above: Len's Dad as a boy.

See the one on the right there? I spent half my childhood shut in that bastard. And you know what? When I was a little kid I used to come home from school and do just what we're doing right now. I'd be able to see my mum at the sink and I'd shout for her to open the door. Daft innit? It's like I can see her now.' It wasn't daft because I could see her myself.

All we could really see was a passageway of doors, the only open one giving us an angled view into that tiny kitchen. Yet between the two of us we mentally filled the place with laughter and tears as he remembered the reality and I conjured up what he'd shared with me.

As we drove away from Kent Street Lenny said, 'Well, now you've seen the place I've done a lot of talking about, but between you and me I don't think it was a good idea coming back,' and he never said another word until we got back to Strahan Road.

Right: Len's Dad with Len (left) and Linda.

Strangely enough Lenny never wanted to make any mileage out of his traumatic and painful childhood. Like the cancer that cut short his life, it was the hand he had been dealt. He'd faced it, then put it behind him, so as far as he was concerned it was a part of his life that could be of no interest to anyone else. So if any impression is given that he might have wanted sympathy or used this painful period as any sort of excuse, then the fault is mine for asking him to hold nothing back

An Extract From
THE GUV'NOR by Lenny McLean

I came home from school one day. It must have been winter because it was dark and freezing cold. As I came up the last flight of stairs my little brother Kruger was huddled on the floor by the door. This was Raymond, but we all called him Kruger because when he was a baby he looked just like an old German man who lived downstairs. Anyway, he's crying, his nose is running, and he's wet himself. I put my arm round him and I asked, 'What's up, mate, did you think we'd all left you?' He sort of nodded and said, 'There's no one in.' I knew that or he wouldn't have been sitting there. Then we both jumped as the lift door opened right beside us and there was Jim Irwin, who had appeared like a fucking genie from a lamp.

'What's up with you, cry-baby?' he said to Kruger.

'I think I've wet meself,' he said and I felt my stomach turn over. That was definitely the wrong thing to say.

Irwin flung the door open, grabbed him by the collar, and dragged him inside the flat. He stripped him naked and started slapping his bare backside with his open hand. That wasn't enough, so he took his belt off and used that. I could see the buckle cutting into Kruger's skinny little body so I tried to grab the belt. It earned me such a punch in the head I went cross-eyed for a minute. But I had another go and Jim kicked me twice without releasing his hold on my brother. I wasn't counting but he must have hit him about 30 times, and then he threw him on to the bed.

While he was being beaten Kruger was screaming, but now he was all scrunched up on the bed, lying so quietly I thought he must be dead. When Mum came in, Irwin told her not to go near him. 'Rose, luv, I've had to give him a bit of a smack for wetting himself, so leave him to think about it in bed until the morning.'

When we all went to bed at about six, I looked under the covers and his body and bottom were all covered in bloody welts. He just lay there, white faced and shivering. Four years old and beaten worse than a dog. I got into bed and cuddled him, and do you know what that brave little lad said?

'I'm sorry I wet meself, Lenny,' he said. He was sorry – he was smashed to bits and was sorry for causing trouble.

I could hear that bastard laughing in the other

room, and I thought, 'I'm going to get you hurt for what you've done.' As young as I was, I could take whatever he could dish out, but I couldn't bear to see any of the others get it.

I lay there for hours still holding little Kruger. I heard the telly shut down, we had one by then, and I think it used to go off at about eleven in those days. Still, I lay there until I was sure everyone was asleep. Then I woke up my brother, told the others to keep quiet, dressed us both and sneaked out of the flat. My mate Alfie had a go-kart made from an old pram, and he used to keep it tucked behind the rubbish bin on the ground floor. I got that out really quietly, laid Kruger on it and, pulling him along with a bit of string, set off to take him to my mum's mum, Nan Campion.

It wasn't that far, but it seemed like miles. It started to snow and it was pitch dark. About halfway there I saw a copper but I pulled the cart up an alley and hid until he'd gone by. Don't ask me why — it was just instinct, just something you always did. Eventually, we got there and the house was all dark but I banged on the door until I got Nan out of bed.

My eldest sister Linda was there, because Nan had taken her in when Dad died to make it easier for Mum.

My mum's brother, Uncle Fred Campion, was there, too. He was halfway down the stairs in his underpants, hair all sticking up. What a diamond of a man. From the day my father died that lovely man bought all our Christmas presents, right up until we were grown up. He never married, just looked after Nan and Linda. Now he's an old man and things have turned round. Nan's dead and Linda looks after him. I haven't seen him for years — you lose touch as you get older, but I'll always love him for what he did for us. Anyway, when they saw the mess Kruger was in there was hell to pay. Looking back, the scenes in my head are like fast-forwarding a video, all rushing and blurry.

I'm put to bed, Kruger's taken to hospital, the police are called and, best of all, as I hoped would happen, Nan sent for her brother, Jimmy Spinks. Why he wasn't called in years ago I don't know. I suppose Mum was ashamed of becoming involved with Jim Irwin and kept what went on to herself. Now I'd let the cat out of the bag, not for myself but for my brother.

My great-uncle Jimmy was one of the toughest men to come out of Hoxton. He was about 21 stone and 5ft 9in, built like an ox, with powerful arms and shoulders, and a fighting reputation that couldn't be bettered in those days. I'll tell you more about him in a bit, but right then, when he saw for himself what had been done to that child, he tore straight round our flat like a raging bull. The police had already been up to the flat and Mum had talked them out of prosecuting, so I expect that smug bastard thought he'd got away with it again. That was until Uncle Jim came through the door. I learned all this afterwards. He didn't knock, he actually punched the door open.

Jim Irwin just had time to come out of the sitting-room before he was battered, semi-conscious, back in again. Now remember, Uncle Jim was twice his age, but Irwin didn't stand a chance. As he got to his feet those massive fists put him down again, then out came the cut-throat razor. Whether he would have used it we'll never know, but he was more than capable and it wouldn't have been the first time. Mum, however, pleaded with him to give Irwin another chance. For Mum's sake he didn't use the razor, but told him to 'Fuck off' there and then or he'd, as Uncle Jim put it, 'end up with a face like mine'.

Now that was a threat because Uncle Jim's face had so many knife and razor scars that it looked like a map of the Underground. Irwin got the message. He might have been the business when it came to knocking the bollocks out of little babies, but fronted up by a real man that gutless coward went to pieces and buggered off without arguing.

Uncle Jimmy was a very tough man and in his day was the Guv'nor of Hoxton. He was what they called a 'ten-man job', because to bring him down you would have to go ten-handed or turn up with a shooter. I've got to say I've heard that said about myself and I'm proud to think I've inherited that from him. He was a very hard man — a tearaway. He was in one of the gangs that worked the horse racing circuits, running protection. He used to mind the bookies and the number one bookmaker in that area at the time was a

Opposite: Lenny's great uncle Jimmy Spinks. Reg Kray said of him, 'Anyone taking Spinks on had to resort to blades and iron bars to compensate for their own inadeqacy.'

Above: **The early days in Hoxton.**

Jewish bloke called Lasky. Jimmy would mind all the other bookmakers on the street corners in that area. That was his block and he was a force to be reckoned with.

I looked up to Jimmy when I was a young boy. I used to love seeing him because he always gave us money and in those days there was little about. He always had money. Jimmy was very powerful and menacing, but a loving man to all his family, and always dressed immaculately – white shirt, tie, the big hat, the Crombie overcoat, and the pinstriped suit – the typical Al Capone gangster. He was the main man.

I remember when my father died, Jimmy went round all the pubs and had a collection for my mum. That was in 1953 and he raised a load of money and handed over every penny. I think that probably helped to feed us until Irwin appeared on the scene. I don't forget things like that, even though I was only five years old.

CHAPTER 3

Lenny The Fighter

Ask anyone who's seen me fight. Does Lenny
ever back off? No. He keeps moving all the
time. Does Lenny ever react or flinch when
he's taken a punch? No. He feels nothing. Just
dishes it out. Anyone taking me on was
putting a loaded gun to their head, but it
never stopped them trying because they
thought, 'One day he'll be put down and I
want to be the one who does it.'

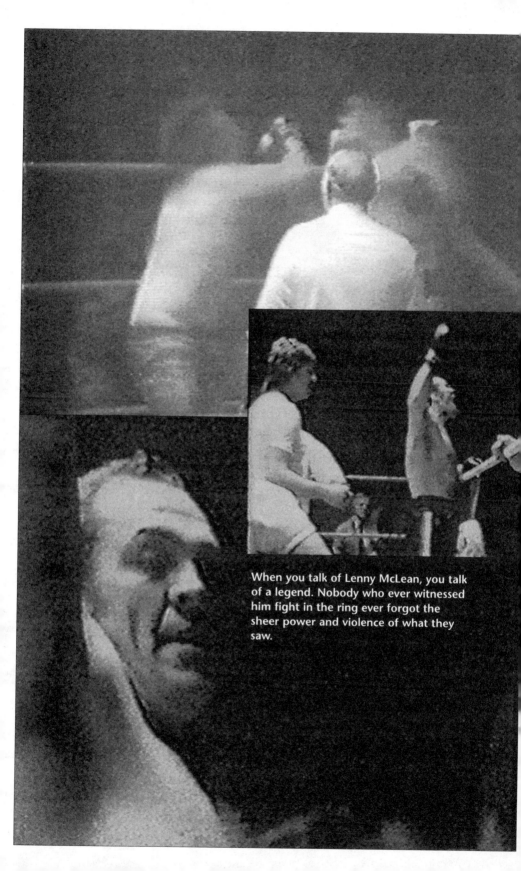

When you talk of Lenny McLean, you talk of a legend. Nobody who ever witnessed him fight in the ring ever forgot the sheer power and violence of what they saw.

LENNY WAS AN unbelievable fighter – and this was more to do with what was inside him than just down to that incredible physique. After all there are lots of very big fellas around but few if any had what Len had. Almost every point of his life that you touch on is linked in some way to Irwin and the brutality he subjected that little boy to. And if Lenny had ever given this serious thought I'm sure he would have hated being linked to that man for life. But it's an inescapable fact that much of his personality was formed in those years that he lived under the same roof as Irwin. In his own words, 'After what that beast did to me, no man was ever going to hurt me again,' and they never did.

Dishing out punishment is one thing – taking it another, and no matter what punch, kick or gouge was directed at him, he never flinched or backed away. There

Left: **Lenny never flinched or backed away from any punch or kick directed at him.**

is video footage of Len fighting 'Mad Gypsy' Bradshaw and thirty seconds of this often pops up fronting some programme on the horrors of unlicensed boxing. Moments before he was smashed into unconsciousness that lasted almost fifty minutes, this Bradshaw, no lightweight, nutted Len full on the forehead. He might as well have hit him with a feather duster because Len took the blow without moving half an inch. His only reaction was to wipe a hand across his face.

The man didn't seem to know what pain was – not physical pain anyway. When it came to inflicting

Below: **Lenny in the ring.**

punishment, and I'm quoting again, 'Every punch I ever gave was for that little baby I used to be, who couldn't fight back.' This combination was something that couldn't be beaten. Outside impervious to hurt – inside a burning but controlled anger. Add the incredible speed of his fists and you're looking at a machine made for violence. Yet you had to be at the end of those speeding fists to appreciate how fast they were.

We were larking about one day and he gave me a shove. Eleven stone four soaking wet, I squared up to him saying, 'C'mon then if you fancy your chances.' I swear to God I never saw his hands move, as in the blink of an eye, he lightly tapped me on the forehead and chin before stepping back laughing and saying, 'Stick to the books my son, 'cos if you fronted me up in a real situation you'd have been spark out before you finished talking.' I believed him.

He pulled a similar stunt when he was invited to give advice to a supposed bare-knuckle fighter for a TV programme. This turned out to be a con against the programme makers, but at the time everyone believed it was genuine, including Len who gave it one hundred percent. On camera he was explaining how this fella should react, then obviously deciding that actions were more effective than words, suddenly rained a flurry of feigned punches at this guy. His fists were a blur and the fear-stricken look on the con man's face was, and still is, a joy to watch on video, and well deserved for trying to make Lenny look a mug by associating him with the scam.

I always found it a paradox that he often emphasised

how much he hated violence yet at the same time was one of the most well known exponents of just that. But at the same time I can understand how he got involved in this world. He wasn't educated in an academic way, he'd no trade and at a time in his life when he was looking for direction he was offered a way of earning easy money (as far as he was concerned). When he found that this way of life put 'steam on the table' and a large helping of gravy, there was no turning back.

A Tribute From
Mick Theo,
BRITISH HEAVYWEIGHT CHAMPION 1991

I first met Lenny about seventeen years ago when I went on the door at Camden Palace. As he would say, he took me under his wing and from then on we were mates right up until the end.

Anyone working the doors in clubs or pubs becomes a target for any likely lads looking to make a name for themselves. But when word got around that Big Lenny was behind me I hardly got any aggravation. That was the power of the man – put his name up and a lot of trouble was stopped before it even started.

I'll never forget the morning I had to break some bad news to him. The night before he'd had a problem with a guy at the Hippodrome and word got back to me that he had died. I knew it was too early for Lenny to know anything about it so I got on the phone and put him in the picture and warned him to expect

Above: One of Len's oldest friends was Mick Theo. He was Britain's Strongest Man, and they worked together at the Camden Palace.

a visit from the police. He didn't believe me and thought I was winding him up. As if the possibility of facing a murder charge was anything to joke about. That was a bad day for everyone that knew him, but he got justice in the end even though it took eighteen months behind the door before it was all cleared away.

He faced that and many other experiences that would have destroyed most people with the same courage that he faced his final days.

I'll remember him as a good guy who was always there for me.

An Extract From
THE GUV'NOR by Lenny McLean

Finsbury Park, Rainbow Theatre, Monday, and I was taking it easy in the dressing room. Everybody else was flapping around, but I, who was going to do the business, couldn't give a bollocks. I just let them all get on with it.

I closed my eyes for a minute, nice and relaxed, then I heard this voice beside me say, 'Hello, son.' I thought I was dreaming, until I opened my eyes and there was Jim Irwin. 'They said it would be all right if I popped in and had a word.' I jumped up to get hold of him and he flinched back, then I thought of Mum, sat down again and just looked at the man. I couldn't smash into him, and nothing I could say would ever communicate the contempt and hatred I had for him. 'Don't call me "son", don't even think of me as your son, just fuck off out of my sight.'

He was not the man he was — he had lost weight and was looking old. He just stood there with a funny look on his face. Doesn't the mind work in strange ways? For a tiny second, I felt sorry for him, then it was gone and I screamed at him, 'Get out of here now, you bullying, gutless bastard, and never come near me again!' I turned my head away and when I looked back he'd gone and I haven't seen him since. He might even be dead and, if he is, he'll be a million miles away from Mum and Dad, because a slag like that has got to be burning in hell.

BOXING

at the
RAINBOW THEATRE
FINSBURY PARK LONDON
on

11th September 1978

In aid of CHILDRENS MUSCULAR DYSTROPHY & AUTISTIC CHILDREN

Featuring a 10 x 3m

CLOSE ENCOUNTER FOR A THIRD TIME for the UNOFFICIAL

HEAVYWEIGHT CHAMPIONSHIP of GREAT BRITAIN

Lennie 'Boy' McLean

THE COOLEST DADDY OF THEM ALL

Roy 'Pretty Boy' Shaw

WILL THE MEAN MACHINE REGAIN THE TITLE

Steve 'Columbo' Richards	Tommy Adams	John McDade
v	v	v
Steve Armstrong	Micky May	Danny Woods
Ralph Harris	Terry Scrutton	Micky Davison
v	v	v
Danny Chippendale	John Ricky	To be announced

Doors open at 7.00 p.m.   Boxing commences 8.00 p.m.

Tickets: £12.50 £10.00 £7.50 £5.00 £2.50

AVAILABLE FROM

C. PINI 01 837 6891

DIXIE DEAN 01 253 8072

RAINBOW BOX OFFICE

HENRY BROWN 01 739 7582

The promotional poster for the third and final bout with Roy Shaw.

One of our runners had sneaked into Shawey's dressing room. He was only a kid so no one took any notice. He told us that Roy was walking up and down looking thoughtful. It sounded like he wasn't so confident this time.

Then Gary Glitter started belting out of the speakers, 'Come on, come on', and I knew Shawey was on his way down. I gave him enough time to start wondering whether I'd bottled out, then I gave it the big entrance. It wasn't that far down the gangway to the ring, but I seemed to go down it in slow motion. I could see Roy bobbing up and down in the ring; the crowd was roaring and all eyes were on me. I stopped for a second and looked all round at the punters screaming for blood and I thought, 'You lot have come to see a fight ... well, this one you won't forget,' then I climbed through the ropes.

I looked to my left and a row of hard faces stared back up at me. I gave them thumbs down and glanced to the right. There was Arthur, and all around him his tartan mob were cheering and shouting remarks. I gave them a wave, swivelled round, and fixed my eyes on Roy Shaw. He turned his back on me and shrugged off his robe that had 'Mean Machine' in big letters on the back. He didn't look so cool now and I could see by his eyes that he thought he was going to do this upstart in the first few seconds. Some hope!

We were introduced. The bell went and he tore at me, his arms going like pistons. He was trying to finish me quick.

He got about four good belts in but two of mine sent him backwards and I kept him going with left and rights to the body. A surprised look flickered across his face and he went down. He got back up, but now he was on the defensive. I've got him ... I battered him a full circuit of the ring, then as he gave me two feeble jabs he wasn't quick enough with his guard and I chopped him to the side of his head. For a fraction of a second he seemed to stop dead, then I hit him again and again and again. Solid punches, every one to the head. The ninth one put him down. I've never fought anyone before or since who could've taken half what he did and stayed on their feet.

The promoter didn't have to worry. Roy was spark out. He wouldn't need any more to finish him.

His team dragged him to his feet and pulled him into the corner, and as he came to he was trying to carry on. I could hear Joe Carrington shouting, 'It's over, Roy, it's over,' and Roy was shaking his head saying, 'Who done me, who done me?' I laughed inside and thought, 'I done you ... Lenny McLean has fucking well done you.'

I swung round to the crowd — they were going wild. I held my arms high and shouted to them all, 'Who's the Guv'nor?' and a great cheer went round the place. Again, I threw my arms in the air and bellowed out, 'Who's the Guv'nor?' and the roar was deafening. 'Lenny ... Lenny ... Lenny ...' Everybody's on their feet. My mob's going crazy and even Roy's lot are clapping and cheering. I'd done it.

I never really set out to become the Guv'nor, but now I was, and nobody would ever take that away from me.

I was in the dressing room afterwards, sitting there having a cup of coffee and relaxing after my couple of minutes' effort, when I looked up and two blokes walked in. I thought I recognised them but couldn't place their faces. Then the penny dropped and I went, 'Fuck me, it's Superman.' They both laughed at that and introduced themselves – Christopher Reeve and Gene Hackman. Can you believe it, these two superstars wanted me to sign a programme for them? They congratulated me on the win and we had some photos taken. Years after, Christopher Reeve broke his back in a terrible accident and was paralysed. I hear he's slowly on the mend and I just want him to know that Big Lenny says keep fighting and one day, please God, you'll be back up on your feet.

A Tribute From
Paddy Monoghan,
CHAMPION BARE-KNUCKLE FIGHTER

My old pal Lenny McLean and myself go back a long, long way, yet it seems like no time since we first met. That was years ago when he came not only to see one of my fights, but to take on a fight himself, in a place called The Barn, notorious as a venue for bare-knuckle fighting. The heavyweight who turned up that day bottled out when he was told his opponent was to be the (then) young Lenny.

My fight went ahead – I won it and collected my meagre purse, then headed straight for home in Abingdon, Oxfordshire. From that day, Lenny and me struck up a close friendship and I've always had and always will have the greatest possible respect for the man.

During those early days after we'd both just won a couple of fights in Stow-on-the-Wold, Lenny phoned me to say that he'd just been matched with Sean Mcaffery, the Irish bare-knuckle Heavyweight Champion. This bout was to take place at the forthcoming Newmarket Horse Traders' Fair, and he was on the blower to let me know that he'd put my name down against Benny Lafferty, the Irish Middleweight Champion.

Both Mcaffery and Lafferty were unbeaten, but then so were Lenny and me. We both accepted the challenges and Lenny told me to make sure I trained hard for this one – not that I really needed telling. Right up until the fight date he rang me regularly, not just to say hello, but enquiring about my fitness and reminding me to train hard. He even wanted me to go to London and train with him so he could keep an eye on me, but I assured him I was working out every day and was in the best shape I'd ever been in.

By the time I left for the Horse Fair I'd begun to wonder why Lenny was taking such an interest in my training and fitness. When I arrived he greeted me with his usual bear hug. He was already kitted out in his fight gear tracksuit bottoms and tee shirt and he said, 'Paddy my old son, how you feeling? You sure you've been training hard for this Lafferty geezer?' I assured him I was in the best shape I'd ever been and without

Above: Paddy Monoghan, bare-knuckle fighter and lifelong friend of Lenny. Len taught Paddy one of the most important lessons to be learned in the fighting game: 'Side bets my son – I learned a long time ago that it's side bets that bring in the real dough.'

being cocky, reckoned I'd do my bloke in the second round. He said, 'Good boy. Now don't you let me down.' Which puzzled me a bit, because it was nothing to Lenny if I won or lost.

Later, as we got changed and the two of us were shadow boxing to warm up, my curiosity got the better of me and I said to Lenny, 'I know we're good pals and we always wish the best for each other, but why the fuck are you so concerned with how fit I am for this Lafferty fella? I mean, you've seen what I can do, I'm going to fucking murder him.'

Lenny reacted with that big belly laugh of his, tapped the side of his nose and said, 'Make sure you do then, and I'll tell you why later.'

I won't bore you with all the fight details such as bobbing and weaving, hooks and uppercuts – all the blood, sweat and gore. But I will say that bare-knuckle fighting is the toughest game in the world. Every punch you give and take is bone crunching against bone.

With Lafferty in such a state that he wasn't fit to carry on, I won my fight slightly over my estimated time, when it was stopped at the beginning of the third round. Two deep cuts over each eye and a rip in his forehead blinded the poor bastard with his own blood, so that he couldn't see where the next punch was coming from. I was doing my job without mercy, but I felt the fight should have been stopped earlier. So now with Lafferty beaten for the first time in his career the Irish Middleweight Champion had to come to terms with defeat and I collected the winner's purse. In fact it was the most I'd ever collected up until then – £150.

After the fight Lenny was the first to congratulate me. He punched the air saying, 'Well done me ol' son, you've just won me five hundred smackers.' The penny dropped and I realised why he was so concerned about my fitness and that I trained hard for this fight.

'What??? I get £150 for doing the fighting and you get £500 for doing sweet FA???'

He just grinned. 'Yeah, innit a nice easy way to earn a bit of scratch? And it'll be the same after I've gone to work on Lavatory, or whatever 'is name is. Side bets my son – I learned a long time ago that it's the side bets that bring in the real dough, so I'll be collecting my dosh from them mugs who thought I was going to get beat.' It turned out that Lenny had 'run a book' with a bunch of horse traders who'd put their money on the previously unbeaten champion Benny Lafferty.

Soon after it was time for Lenny's. He was a giant of a man towering over Big Lenny, but that wasn't to be the case for long because in the first round Lenny knocked him spark out with a short right hander and, typical for him, never even broke into a sweat.

So Lenny not only picked up his own winner's purse, but a bundle on mine and a bigger one in side bets on himself. But as we left Newmarket together, he put his arm on my shoulder and said, 'Hey Paddy, I've been thinking.'

'Yeah Lenny, what about?'

He said, 'You know you said you only got £150 for your fight and you won me 500 smackers for doing FA? Well that don't sound right somehow.' And with that he peeled off £250 in notes from the wad of cash and shoved it into my hand.

I'm saying, 'Nah Lenny, it's your dosh, you won it fair and square,' but he refused to take it back. Just said 'Shadapp'. That was the sort of man he was. He'd rather give than take and never expected anything in return.

Though I didn't know it at the time the last meeting I would have with my old friend was at Ron Kray's funeral. Once the formalities were over and our respects paid, it was time for old associates and friends to acknowledge each other. In particular I was looking around for Big Lenny, but couldn't see him. Then, as my group walked away from the graveside, a voice came to my attention as it got nearer. 'Hey Paddy ... Hey Pad ... Oi Paddy.' Then I felt a great big hand, the size of a shovel, clasping me by the shoulders from behind. I didn't recognise the hand at first but there was no mistaking that deep growling cockney gravel voice as it came out with 'Paddy Monaghan, I've got ten grand that says I can take you spark-out 'ere and now.' The laugh that followed was just as unmistakable as his voice: 'Gotcha! Ha Ha Ha!' I turned round to find my dear old pal standing like a colossus in front of me. The one and only Lenny McLean.

We embraced like a couple of long-lost brothers, then we stepped back and sized each other up. I said, 'Wotcher, me ol' son, you're looking well.'

'Yeah, you too. How about us both making a comeback eh?' Still with that big, warm, unforgettable smile he put a friendly arm across my shoulder and said, 'Come on, Paddy, I want you to meet someone.' He guided me to a tall figure of a man. 'Paddy, meet Peter Gerrard, my book man. Me and him are working on my life story and it's going to be a blinder.'

He began to tell Peter more about him and me. He said, 'I've bin telling this little Irishman to make the move here into town for years. He could easily get sorted here and make a good livin' hanging about with me, but he won't leave that fucking barnyard.' Then he said, 'I'll tell you something, Paddy, that'll do you a bit of good. Put yourself up for a bit of acting like I'm doing now, 'cos it's money for old rope. Gimme the word and I can get you into the game. I know you can do it and it's a piece of piss compared to all that fighting we've had to do in the past to earn a crust.'

Then Lenny invited me back to his pub, appropriately named The Guvnor's, along with others who attended Ronnie Kray's funeral. He was still bending my ear with the acting proposition and was even suggesting taking me down to Pinewood Studios with him.

As I headed home later that evening, not knowing that was to be the last time I'd see my old pal alive, I've got to be honest and say that he'd planted a seed in my mind and I began to think more seriously about that acting business. Many times after that when we were chatting on the phone he'd bring the subject up. Finally, with nothing to lose, I decided to give it a go. But I'd left it too late, for my old pal died of cancer in the summer of '98.

As I attended his funeral on August 5th 1998 I felt a great sense of loss. We had a bond and I loved the man like a brother.

With his work on the book Peter had done Lenny proud and the big guy knew it. During one of my telephone chats with Lenny he told me he had the greatest confidence in Peter because, 'He got to know me as Lenny McLean the Man, and not just Lenny McLean the Fighter.' He told me he'd started out as his biographer but had since become his friend. 'An' I'll tell yer this now Paddy. When my book comes out it's gonna be a bestseller... I'll betcha.'

I'm glad I didn't put money against it because you was right Lenny ... you was right me ol' son.

Big Lenny was a man of great contrasts, despite all those 'hard-man' stories that you read about him, and I could tell you quite a few of my own. He was a very caring and considerate person and I'm proud to have been his associate and his friend.

London has produced some of the hardest men in the world, but you can believe me when I tell you they never came any harder than Lenny McLean. He truly was, and always will be, THE GUV'NOR OF ALL GUV'NORS.

Being a bare-knuckle fighter is the toughest trade in the world. It separates the men who tear up the rulebook from the boys who abide by it. Every bare-knuckle fighter worth his salt from Chicago to Timbuktu has heard about Lenny McLean. He will always be looked up to one way or another.

Respect cannot be bought. It is something that can only be earned, and he most certainly earned mine.

A Tribute From
Johnny Nash,
BUSINESSMAN

When Lenny McLean died, he left a big vacuum; for Lenny wasn't just big in stature, he was big in every way, and I am proud to say that he was a good and special friend of mine. It was an honour knowing the man.

Above: Johnny Nash, one of Lenny's oldest friends, who stood by him whether in the ring or out.

On the few occasions that we worked together, we did have some laughs. Lenny was quite funny, the way he put things and the phrases he used, and as I am quick-witted myself the day and the work would be full of laughs. Now and then, when those times flood back to me, I have to smile!

After the years he spent fighting and being the Guv'nor, he turned his hand to acting. It was Mike Reid who planted the seed in his mind, so with his perseverance, charm and ability he got his Equity card, and whether it was The Knock *or* Lock Stock *he was without a doubt being himself, he was a natural. Not only in London, but up and down the country he earned everybody's respect for something else he had put his hand to.*

Lenny was very brave, and in death he knew the score. He met his death head on, and one of the last times I saw him he told me that he was focussed for it. Focussed or not, he never gave up the fight – he never had it in him to do that. In his 49 years he left a big impact: I think he crammed enough in his life for someone twice his age, and he was just changing into another gear when he was struck down with cancer, a fight nobody can win. It saddened me so much because he fought so hard, but to me and anybody who really knew him – they are that much richer.

I myself shall remember him as a man of his word and of solid values. Yes, he did leave a big space behind, but he also left a lot of good memories to fill it! He was something else.

God bless you my friend.

Your Pal Johnny Nash

An Extract From
Nosher, by Nosher Powell

Let me tell you about Lenny. He was probably the most frightening man I ever knew, but we were mates. We go back a long time, Lenny and me. Picture a man as tall as me, but weighing over twenty stone, with a forty-inch waist and a sixty-inch chest. He was huge. He was also very dangerous when he got angry, and tended to walk through doors rather than open them. His exploits became the stuff of legend.

Lenny always showed me the highest respect, and I showed him the same. I always knew I could count on him, just as he could count on me if he ever needed to.

That time came with this geezer Dave and his mates who were going to stitch me up in my own car park.

You'll have gathered by now that Lenny was a useful man to have in your own corner, especially if that corner was a tight one.

He took my call. "Ello, Nosh, 'ow are yer?' His voice sounded like rusty nails being shaken in a metal tin.

'Fine, Lenny, fine. But I got a problem.'

He never said to me 'why?' or 'what?' He simply said: 'Where's the meet, Nosh?'

I told him. 'My gaff. The Prince of Wales car park, Garratt Lane.'

'What time?'

'Four o'clock tomorrow afternoon,' I said.

'I'll be there.'

Prompt at four I drove into the car park. Right opposite across the road was a firm dealing in used tyres — and there was Lenny's huge bulk, casually leaning against the fence.

But my immediate concern now was Big Dave, sitting on the bonnet of his shining BMW. Studying his fingernails, cool as a cucumber despite his bruised face. When he saw me coming, he stood up and signalled with one hand. Over on one side I saw an old van, and faces peering out of the windows.

As I walked towards him three big pikeys got out of the van and started towards me.

They joined up with the smoothie, and now there were four of them walking in line just like that scene in Reservoir Dogs.

This was it. I knew I'd been right, and I wasn't even tooled up because I only ever used my fists. But that was the moment when another figure came into the equation — Lenny materialised from around the fence, to stroll across to my car and lean against it quietly with his arms folded.

Christ, you should have seen their faces! The first pikey — Eric was his name, a tough local gypsy boy — turned round to Mr Smooth and hissed: 'You c—t! You want to get us fucking deaded?' And whack! He gave him one across the chops, and Dave went sprawling.

Eric looked past me, at the figure leaning casually against my car. 'Sorry, Lenny, sorry! We never knew the SP or we wouldn't be here. If it's about the three grand he's got in his pocket — listen, we're out of here!'

With that the three of them beat a hasty retreat and scrambled back into the van — only to find their way barred by Lenny's huge bulk. He just stood there, with one hand extended.

'What? What is it, Lenny?'

Lenny uttered a single word. 'Expenses!'

Staring terrible personal retribution in the face tends to focus the mind like nothing else. Eric pulled out a wad, and threw it at him. 'Sure, Lenny. Sorry, sorry ...' And, whoosh, they were away like greased lightning.

Meantime, my geezer was getting to his feet. 'My money?' I said. He was already pulling out a roll. I counted out two grand, added a further monkey for the inconvenience, threw the remaining five hundred quid at him, and walked off. I never did see that bastard again.

That evening Lenny and I went on to celebrate with a slap-up steak dinner at Jack's Place down by Battersea heliport, a restaurant where a lot of faces used to gather.

He said: 'Nosher, you'd have done the same for me.'

I told him: 'Yeah, course I would. But you deserve a few quid for this night's work.' He wound up with six hundred pounds in his pocket, and worth every penny of it.

Over the last brandy, Lenny said: 'Any time you've got a problem, Nosh, just phone me.' If Lenny's friends had a problem, it became his problem. That's the kind of man he was.

My Very Best Regards

Nathan Powell

A Tribute From
John Huntley,
FORMER MALE MODEL, FIGHTER, AND CLOSE FAMILY FRIEND

I knew Lenny for the best part of 22 years. I first met him at the boxing gym where I used to train. From that first meeting I knew I was in the presence of someone very special.

The first thing you notice is his awesome appearance. But the more time you spent with Lenny, the more you grew to know that he was quite unique. He had everything: presence, charisma, wit, charm, the lot.

The most tragic conclusion to Lenny's life is that it ended when people started to notice that there was much more to him than his physical appearance suggested. With the massive success of his autobiography which was the number one bestseller for a record number of weeks, and the pending film of his life story which has already been tipped as the film of the year, he was on the brink of becoming a superstar in the motion picture business.

The American TV companies would have loved him for his sense of humour – all the one-liners and never-ending tales of his life. He was a marketing company's dream. The media would have discovered a gold mine and Lenny would have been catapulted to world stardom.

I said in my speech at Lenny's funeral that there would never be another Lenny McLean, he was a one-off. He really was the last of the real tough guys.

It was a privilege to have known Lenny, and an honour to have had him as my closest friend.

Lenny with John Huntley. Two fighters with real respect for each other.

BARE FIST FIGHTING.

The ancient Greeks made it part of their original Olympics 3,000 years ago. In 19th Century England, it was said that a third of the Houses of Parliament was taking lessons in it.

BARE FIST FIGHTING.

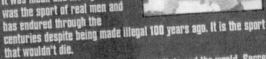
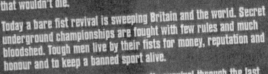

It was mean and bloody but it was the sport of real men and has endured through the centuries despite being made illegal 100 years ago. It is the sport that wouldn't die.

Today a bare fist revival is sweeping Britain and the world. Secret underground championships are fought with few rules and much bloodshed. Tough men live by their fists for money, reputation and honour and to keep a banned sport alive.

This video tells the story of the sport's survival through the last century and the real bare fist fighters reveal the secrets surrounding this illegal form of boxing. Candid footage from actual bare fist fights and narration from the UK's Bare Fist Champion, Lennie Mclean, form a programme which is informative, shocking and always close to the knuckle.

'The hardest man in britain', Lennie 'The Guv'nor' McLean is a former UK bare-knuckle champion and winner of 2,000 bare fist fights. Lennie is soon to be made the subject of a major feature film.

"One of the best street fighter I have ever seen" Ronnie Kray
"He's a legend in his own lifetime" Reggie Kray

Directed and produced by David Monaghan & Heidi Easton-Bennett.

NTV ENTERTAINMENT
Bedford Chambers,
The Piazza,
Covent Garden, London
WC2E 8HA

A David Monaghan Production for NTV
Entertainment Ltd.
© 1996 NTV Entertainment Limited.
℗ 1996 NTV Entertainment Limited.
Running Time: 54 minutes approx.

18 Suitable only for persons of 18 years and over
Not to be supplied to any person below that age

VPRC
VIDEO PACKAGING REVIEW COMMITTEE

5 022053 015713

BARE FIST

THE SPORT THAT WOULDN'T DIE

18

REAL FISTS, REAL FIGHTS, REAL MEAN

GENUINE BARE FIST FIGHTS FROM AROUND THE WORLD

PRESENTED BY
LENNIE "THE GUV'NOR" McLEAN, CHAMPION BARE FIST FIGHTER

Lenny was a street fighting legend. This video calls him the hardest man in Britain – some would say the hardest man in the world,

A Tribute From
Joe Pyle,
PROMOTER AND BUSINESSMAN

I used to manage and promote the original Guv'nor, Roy Shaw. At the time, Roy was unbeaten and unbeatable. He was taking on challenges and the first thing I would ask was: 'Can you sell at least £6,000 worth of tickets?' If they couldn't, they didn't get the fight. Roy was riding a crest, then along came a young fellow from Hoxton. His name was Lenny McLean. I had never heard of him. Roy had never heard of him. We took up Lenny McLean's challenge. After two fights and a win each, a return was arranged and Roy walked straight into a right-hander. Lenny became the Guv'nor. Since that time we became friends. Lenny was a great guy with a lot of respect. One look at Lens pugilistic features and one could see what he had come through. He was a good pal to me and I knew both sides of him, as a fighter and a gentleman. Funny – he reminds me of the character in the book Of Mice and Men .. his name was Lenny, too.

Right: Joe Pyle, the man resposible for bringing Lenny and Roy Shaw together in the ring.

140

The awesome spectacle of Lenny McLean and Roy Shaw together in the ring.

A Tribute From
Freddie Hills,
WORLD CLASS TRAINER

Lenny came under my wing when he was about twenty-four. I have only ever taken on the best, and this kid was one of the toughest fighters I had ever handled. He was a rough diamond but he wanted to learn, so he listened and did everything I told him without arguing.

Below: Even when pictured with his gym mates – some of the hardest men in the country themselves – Lenny towered above them.

My only regret was that I had not got hold of him when he was sixteen, because without a doubt he would have become a World Champion. I should know because I have trained people like Joe Bugner, Alan Rudkin, Billy Walker, Ken Buchanan, and Chris and Kev, the Finnegan brothers.

He was a lovely boy who looked on me as a father figure in his life and never gave me anything other than respect. Later on he became a fierce man, a terrifying man, but away from the fairgrounds and unlicensed fights, a nice man who always championed the underdog and never forgot his friends.

A Tribute From
Bruce Wells,
FORMER OLYMPIC BOXING CHAMPION

I have been retired from the ring for many years now and my fighting days are well behind me. As they were a few years ago when at the time I worked for a ticket agency. While delivering some tickets to Lenny, a special friend, I was given some abusive treatment from half a dozen likely lads who felt I was too old to show my face in the Hippodrome disco scene and thought it clever to start pushing me around. When Lenny saw what was happening he was at my side in a second and the lads were lucky that the least they got was being forcibly ejected.

That summed up Lenny. He would not suffer disrespect and was there for his friends.

Above: Left to right: Frankie Fraser, Charlie Richardson, Lenny, Jack Lavinsky, Alex Steene, Bruce Wells.

A Tribute From

The Late Alex Steene,

PROMOTER

When you speak of Lenny McLean you speak of a legend. A hard man, a tough man and he proved this over and over again – unbeatable.

I have been associated with some of the best fighters in the world and dealt with all kinds of people, both in the underworld and the upperworld. Yet this man stood out like a beacon.

On my office wall hangs a letter from Muhammad Ali, part of which says, 'Lenny McLean is a man I would like to fight before I retire.' I think that sums up Len's reputation, which even reached America.

Some of our friends, top people in the States, had been to see him fight and came away impressed. He had their highest commendation – respect.

Not only that, he was liked. He had sympatico. He asked for nothing on the way up. Everything he gained was on his own merit.

A Tribute from
Lynda La Plante,
AUTHOR

My interest in boxing began as a child when my father took me to the big fights. It lay dormant for a while when I began my acting career, but rose to the surface again when I became a writer. My first television series was called Widows, *and one of the characters was actually called Boxer. A location manager called Micky was an avid boxing fan, and when he read the script he honed in on me and became a sort of creative mentor of that world. Via Micky I went to every gym, all the pubs and bars frequented by fighters. I went to some of the most bizarre venues. Perhaps the most memorable one took place in a school playing field. My mentor told me that this*

Lynda La Plante.

was not a usual fight but starred the king of the unlicensed world, Lenny McLean.

The ring had been erected in the centre of the field with rows of wooden benches around it. A beer tent and old cricket pavilion was the 'changing room'. I went straight for one of the front-row benches but was told by Micky that it might not be such a good idea and he persuaded me to stand at the back, right at the back of the field, up close to the pavilion steps.

This was all a long time ago, but I will never forget seeing the sparkling array of flash vehicles drawing up, from Rolls Royces to Mercedes, parking alongside old coaches and delivery vans. The punters came in their droves, many propped up the makeshift bar in the booze tent, pints overflowed in their plastic cups and were liberally passed around and there were a few totally inebriated fans before the fights even started. Rock music played at ear-splitting level, and still the spectators poured in, and yet I could see no billboards or posters. Micky, snapping away with his camera 'for location purposes!', looked at me shaking his head. Didn't I understand? This was no ordinary fight, this was the big unlicensed champion of champions bout. I was, he said, with an inordinate amount of pride, about to see the 'The Man' himself, third on the bill was 'the greatest', 'the one and only' – I was about to see Lenny McLean – otherwise known as the Guv'nor – in action.

Two fights got underway, and were over quite quickly. The tension in the field became palpable, as did the human missiles being flung aside from in and around the ring. I now realised why sitting up close was a hazard. Boozed up, some of the spectators were having their own fights around the field, and many tried to get up into the ring: they were hurled out by their collars and the seat of their pants, head first! The number of bouncers was increasing, more and more heavy-shouldered, muscular men were taking up their positions in and around the ring.

Then there was a wait, about ten minutes, before the music built even louder and the bells started to ring. Out came the contender, about six foot four, wearing baggy black shorts and a draped T-shirt and massive black gloves. His name went unheard as the punters screamed, 'LENNY... LENNY... LENNEEEE...' and the screaming voice of the compère, like myself close to the safety of the pavilion, yelled into the microphone to announce the arrival of 'the one and only'... the man we had all been waiting for, THE GUV'NOR. And in a flowing cloak, Lenny McLean strode through the line of bodyguards, knocked one out before he got in the ring, and by the time he did jump in, they were screaming and yelling and more human missiles were flung out of the ropes. The ref bellowed that he wanted a clean fight, no biting, no kicking, no headbutting... Lenny swaggered like a warlord, no one would take his title. He was, he shouted, the one and only GUV'NOR.

The bell rang for round one. I think he might have touched his opponents glove's, I think I recall someone had actually said the weights. I know there was a staggering difference between the massive opponent and Lenny, plus he was also about four inches taller if not more. But the bell I am sure did ring, and the fight was over in under a second. I believe it was a 'clash' of heads! All six foot four of bulk lay at Lenny's feet.

Many years later he remained a legend, and by now I had won awards for **Prime Suspect** *and had formed my own company to produce a television series called* **The Governor,** *which was nothing whatsoever to do with Lenny. I had truthfully not even connected the two titles.* The Governor *was a prison series and the title referred to the Governor of the prison, Barfield. The series starred Janet McTeer as the female Governor.*

My publishers were giving a big press party for their authors to celebrate moving into sumptuous new premises. I was making my way up the big wide red-carpeted stairway when there was a tap on my shoulder. I turned to be confronted by the great man himself. He was elegantly attired in a very cool suit, immaculate shirt and tie. He hemmed me into a corner. I was only about as high as his diamond shirt pin. He glared down at me and wagged his finger. 'That was my title you took, Miss La Plante, that title cost me years of hard graft, and just like that you nicked it!' I was unsure how to respond. Then he shot out his left wrist, his huge fist clenched, and dangling from a wrist the size of my head was a diamond studded bracelet, with each letter spelt out in diamonds – The Guv'nor.

'I'm writing my memoirs,' he said, and he roared with laughter. 'I'm taking my title back from you, it's going to be called The Guv'nor. *Is that all right with you, Miss La Plante? If it isn't, what you going to do about it?' The massive fist tapped my chin. 'I'll tell you what you gonna do about it. Nothing. Right?' Right, I nodded, and he gave me a huge bear hug, kissed me on both cheeks and asked if I had a part for him in any of my series as he was not only a writer but an actor.*

I spent a long time huddled with Lenny that evening. He told me he was going to act in The Knock *and that he had a film on offer. I never saw him again until I watched him on the big screen in* Lock, Stock & Two Smoking Barrels, *and then this massive man was gone. Just before he died, I was able to write and tell him how much I had enjoyed his book and his performance in the film, but sadly I was never able to say goodbye to him in person. I know Lenny died fighting his illness, trying for that knockout punch, but it was stronger than he was, stronger than any opponent. I write this with love and affection, with pride too that I was fortunate enough to know him. It's good to 'read all about him' in his book. I hope it keeps on selling and selling, because no one else will ever be the Guv'nor.*

KENNY MAC PRESENTS AN AFTERNOON OF

BOXING

AT WOODFORD TOWN FOOTBALL CLUB
265 SNAKES LANE WOODFORD GREEN ESSEX
IN AID OF THE LORD TAVERNERS COACHES FOR HANDICAPPED CHILDREN
ON SEPTEMBER 7TH 1986 DOORS OPEN AT 12.00 1ST BOUT 1 O'CLOCK
EXTENDED LICENSE FROM 12 - 6 O'CLOCK

LENNY MEAN McLEAN

'May God have mercy on his soul'

Vs

MAN MOUNTAIN YORK

' I am 24 and 6'7" and 23 stone Lenny has had his day'

CHAPTER 4

Lenny
The Family Man

**I've got a wife and family now and they've
got to be looked after, not just with
money but with some sort of sense of
responsibility. Do I knuckle down to a
regular job, pack up getting into rows, and
take a load of shit from some mug boss?
Or do I go the other way to earn a crust?**

Left: **Lenny with his Val, the single most important thing in his life.**

INVARIABLY MEN don't talk about love or feelings. It's a macho thing – sport, birds, motors, page three – anything rather than show weakness by discussing finer feelings. Granted, I was in the privileged position of being given Lenny's thoughts with no holds barred, but even so without any apology or hint of embarrassment he never tired of telling me how much he loved his Val.

She was never 'The Wife', 'The Missus', 'Her Indoors' or any other term most blokes use. She was always 'My Val'. Time after time he would say after she had left the room, 'My Val – Ain't she lovely? You know what? I've loved her since we were kids and I love her a bit more every day.' This was never said for effect, it was just a simple statement of his feelings. As she'd bring in yet another cup of tea he couldn't help touching her hand or arm with an 'Alright Babe?' or 'Alright Doll?' and as the door would close he'd remind me yet again that she was 'His Val and lovely', then back to the business of the book.

As an outsider I could see the truth of what Len often said, that Val was his life and his strength. I could also see that she was his motivation to move forward all the time. He wanted her to have the best of everything and the same for his kids. He spoke with pride whenever he mentioned his son and daughter, Jamie and Kelly. 'Smashing kids, they've never given us a day's trouble.' Full of pride that they had grown up polite and respectful, and were successfully making their way in the world. Satisfied also that because of his efforts over the years they'd never gone without anything, and with him and Val as loving parents had never known the pain he'd had to suffer in those early years.

Above: One of the happiest days of Lenny's life was the day he got married to his Val. 'You know what?' he would say. 'I've loved her since we were kids and I love her a bit more every day.'

Above: Jamie and Kelly – 'Smashing kids, they've never given us a day's trouble.'

A Tribute From
Lenny's Wife, Val

I'm doing a tribute for Lenny, so as hard as it may be I'm going to try.

I was seventeen when I met Lenny. Little did I know that the moment I stepped into the Standard pub in Kingsland Road it would change my life forever. We were inseparable and went everywhere together, and after

159

courting for a year we got married. We had our ups and downs like everybody else does, but we had a strong bond between us, and any upsets were soon forgotten. Later we were blessed with two lovely children Jamie and Kelly, which made our family complete.

There are so many things I could write about Lenny, too many stories to tell, but one thing that sticks in my mind is the day that Lenny finally got his book signing at Dillons in Oxford Street. Lenny was so proud to be signing everybody's book, and I must say that Lenny always knew that the book would be a number one bestseller.

I remember when Lenny was ill, he accepted that the doctors only gave him four months to live. It was me who went to pieces, not Lenny. He was so very brave. The day before Lenny passed away he was still being his normal self, putting his family first, and at ease. That afternoon Lenny called out, 'Val, give me a cuddle because I have got to go now, but I'll be back for you. It's not time for you yet.' And I believe Lenny will be back for me as he always kept his word. Lenny passed away the following day.

I was devastated when I lost Lenny, and I still can't come to terms with it, but there isn't a day goes by when he is not in my heart and my thoughts.

I miss Lenny more than words could ever say.

All my love forever, Lenny.
Your Val XXXXXX

My Dad

You were a dad in a million,
Today it's plain to see,
You did everything for us Dad,
Mum, Jamie and me.

So hard on the outside,
Inside just my Dad,
You did it all and more
Just to make sure that we had.

When I think of how we lost you,
My heart aches and I feel sad,
Any man can be a father
It takes a real man to be a dad.

It goes around my head,
Everything that you went through,
Nothing in life would matter
If I could just have you.

Your loving daughter Kelly XXXX

A Tribute From
Lenny's Son, Jamie

Dad

*There is so much to say about you. There was so much that
people didn't get to see about you. Your kindness, intelligence,
your sense of humour. You had a special gift in which you
could see through people. No one could lie to you. You were the
sharpest man ever and you never feared anyone or anything.*

Above: **Father and son – Lenny with Jamie.**

When you walked in a room you commanded respect from people. You had a presence. Not a day goes by that I don't think of you. It's been two years of not being with you and the pain doesn't get easier. I miss you more than ever.

Anywhere in the world I go people always know a funny story about you. I feel honoured to have had 28 years with you, but it wasn't enough.

Miss you

Jamie

A Tribute From
Karen Latimer,
CLOSE FAMILY FRIEND

I knew Lenny for over 15 years, and we shared a lot of laughs together. He was a big man with a big personality. I started off being Kelly's friend, but over the years I became more and more like part of the family. Lenny looked upon me like one of his own kids and I looked upon Lenny like another father.

When I lived with Lenny and Valerie, I never needed an alarm clock as, of a morning, Lenny would wake me up by literally turning the mattress upside-down, and as my eyes opened, Lenny would be standing there, saying, 'Morning babe, gonna make me a nice cup of tea then?' Then he would clench his fist and say, 'Don't dare tell Val!'

There were so many other stories like that, far too many to

165

Above: Karen Latimer, who Lenny welcomed into his house as one of the family.

tell. I lived with Val, Kelly and Jamie, helping Lenny through his illness and Lenny always remained strong right through to the very end – laughing, singing, and cracking jokes.

Lenny was always very good to me, and I wish he was still here. I love him and miss him so very much. I am so proud to be asked to do this for the book.

166

A Tribute From

Lenny's Brothers and Sisters

Lenny was a real character. Anyone who ever met him never forgot him. He was one of a kind. As a kid he was a real practical joker. He loved Sundays – not that he was particularly religious – but Sunday was the day the Salvation Army used to come round the flats and sing. That was Lenny's cue to heat up a load of pennies which he'd then flick over the balcony. When they picked the pennies up they'd burn their fingers and Lenny would fall about laughing. He was always full of mischief as a kid.

We were all devastated when he was diagnosed with cancer, but he never really complained. One of the things that

Below: **Lenny with his sister Lorraine (left), brother Raymond (middle) and Barry (right).**

would break his heart was the thought of leaving his wife Val, who he adored, and also his Jamie and Kelly. He was a good dad, and they had everything – Lenny made sure of that. It was wonderful that he lived to see his book become a number one bestseller, as he worked so hard for it. We are all very proud of him.

Lenny was very strong, right up until a few days before he passed away. He was still singing his little song, 'Always Look on the Bright Side of Life'.

Everything Lenny achieved in his life was due to hard work and determination. As a kid he wanted to be somebody. Well he was – he was the Guv'nor. Our beloved Mum would have been so proud of her Lenny boy.

God Bless, Lenny.

Above: **Lenny's older sister Linda**

Above the violence and the hustling, the minding and the acting, Lenny's family were by far the most important thing in his life. As long as he could put 'steam on the table', everything was alright.

A Tribute From

The Anderson Family

CLOSE FAMILY FRIENDS

We would like to say how much we miss Lenny. He has been a good friend to the Anderson family, going back many years

In 1982 he donated the money from one of his shows to buy a mobility chair for a boy who needed it. His name was Colin Dodd. Lenny was a good friend to Richie Anderson and he helped the family get through their sad loss of a husband and father.

God Bless, Lenny

From us all.

Above: Early days with Richie Anderson (left) and Arthur Thompson (middle).

Above: Len at a party with Richie Anderson's wife Val.

A Tribute From
Eric and Tracy Hope,
FAMILY FRIENDS

Our friend Lenny, well where can we start? There are so many things, but a couple of stories in particular stick in our minds. For instance, whenever Lenny had an audition he would phone me and say, 'Hello son, I've got us another audition, so you come and pick me up and we'll go together.' So I would drive over and get Lenny from Kent then take him to the West End. When we would reach our destination Lenny would go straight through for his audition so I would then give my name to reception, but they could

171

never find any record of it. So when Lenny had finished, I'd say to him, 'They never had my name down, Len.'

'Never mind, son,' he'd say, 'you'd never be as good as me anyway!' And we'd both have a good laugh.

Lenny was a funny man, and a very brave one. Three months before Lenny passed away we were down Clacton with our families and Lenny knocked one morning and said, 'You coming for a run, son?'

'Not this morning, Len,' I said, 'I'm hungover.' But there was Lenny, diagnosed with lung and brain cancer, going for a run – and I'm not talking round the park, but all the way to Little Clacton and back, at least 14 miles.

Lenny was an extraordinary man who will be greatly missed, especially by our family. What a privilege to have known him.

CHAPTER 5

Lenny In The Dock

Can you imagine being on a murder charge,
and I mean charge, not sentence and you
know you haven't committed the crime? You
live and breathe it every second of the day.
As you wake up in the morning, for one tiny
second it's not there, but count to two and
your head's filled. Murder-life-murder-life, and
that goes on and on until you fall asleep, and
even then it doesn't stop.

REGINA v *LEONARD McCLEAN*

Criminal Appeal Office Ref. No.: 92/1663/Y4

Index No: *NW 2125*

Indictment/Committal for Sentence No: 911240.

ORDER ON THE APPEAL

THE APPELLANT having been [convicted in the Crown Court at *Central Criminal Court on 9 March 1992*] [convicted in the Magistrates' Court and committed for sentence in the Crown Court at _____ on _____].
was on *10 March, 1992, sentenced to 18 months' imprisonment.*

(See Crown Court Record Sheet attached)

THE COURT OF APPEAL CRIMINAL DIVISION on *9th APRIL 1992*

CONSIDERED the appeal against [conviction] and [sentence]

AND HAS *dismissed it,*

Counsel for Appellant: *MR. DAVID WHITEHOUSE, QC.,*

Counsel for Crown:

The Appellant was [not] in custody and was [not] present

Date: *9th APRIL 1992* ....(for the Registrar)

Criminal Appeal Office, Royal Courts of Justice
Strand, London WC2A 2LL

[Form L311]

The murder charge documents that struck into Lenny's heart the fear that he might only see his Val and the kids on visiting days.

DEFENDANT	Male / ~~Female~~ / ~~Company~~		COURT CENTRAL CRIMINAL COURT	Committed on 15.8.91 at Bow Street Mag.Ct. ~~bail~~/in custody)

Leonard McCLEAN
Date of birth 9.4.49

JUDGE
HHJ Pownall QC
~~JUSTICES~~   (15.8.91)
HHJ R. Lowry QC
                (2.3.92)

[Application for bail before trial made at Crown Court on   13.9.91

~~granted~~/refused

Appeared for trial (on bail/in custody/~~otherwise~~)

Tried on 2, 3, 4, 5, 6, 9, 10 March 1992

DEFENCE [Legal Aid/Private]
Counsel   Mr. J. Goldberg QC
                    (15.8.91)
Solicitors
Mr. D. Whitehouse QC) 2.3.92
Miss K. Kahl   )
Ralph Haeems & Co.

[~~change in bail/remand status before verdict (if known) given~~]

Convicted on 9.3.92

[Put back for sentence on bail/in custody]

Sentenced or Order made on
      10.3.92

PROSECUTION
Counsel   Mr. M. Fortune (15.8.91)
Solicitors
Mr. D. Calver-Smith)2.3.92
Mr. D. Lovell-Pank)
C.P.S.

SHORTHAND WRITERS
Newgate Reporters plc

Count	Offence	Plea	Verdict	Sentence or Order
1	Murder	Not Guilty 2.3.92	Not Guilty By direction Count 1 (9.3.92)	[~~Sentence deferred until~~]xx on
3	Causing Grievous Bodily Harm with intent to do grievous bodily harm		Guilty of Assault occasioning actual bodily harm on Count 4 (own confession)	18 Months Imprisonment
4	Inflicting Grievous Bodily Harm		Not Guilty inflicting grievous bodily harm	
			Not Guilty by direction Count 3	

Form 5089

Continue over

FOR SOMEONE of Lenny's intimidating appearance and reputation, going into prison was for him like us ordinary mortals going on holiday. But what made his last spell behind the door hard to take was one, he knew he was innocent, and two the charge was murder, with the strongest possibility that any judge conversant with his reputation would recommend that if found guilty he should serve twenty-five years. Len told me that if he'd gone down with that rec, he couldn't have done it. I doubt that. Having seen how he faced a far greater sentence in the last months of his life, he'd have done the same even if sent down for fifty years.

But at the time the thought of only ever seeing his Val and the kids on visiting days came close to destroying him, even though he kept those feelings inside.

One of the first things he did shortly after we met was to hand me a bundle of legal paperwork and statements with the question, 'Did I do it? You tell me – should I have been done for murder?' I'm no lawyer but I can read and the strongest evidence in these hundreds of pages was that at worst he was guilty of common assault. The facts didn't even come near a manslaughter, let alone murder.

The law says that a murder charge can be reduced once the facts are aired in court, but manslaughter can't be upgraded. So naturally if there are any doubts at all, the higher charge is pushed forward by the prosecutor and any chance of bail goes right out of the window.

Until the day he died Lenny felt that there had been a conspiracy to get him off the streets. Coupled with this he strongly believed the opinion of Professor Gresham, 'The possibility that Gary Humphries died when he was held in a strangle hold by an officer of the law.'

Like himself I read all the statements from ordinary bystanders. Granted Humphries appeared to have the strength of five men, but by all accounts there were more than that trying to wrestle him into a police van. Some of these people actually tried to intervene when they saw the distressed state of Humphries while being held in a neck lock, a number of them shouting, 'Let him go you're killing him.'

It's not my place to retry the pre-trial evidence that put Lenny away, but I find it difficult to understand how even the lowliest clerk couldn't have spotted something was out of order. It might have saved Lenny and his family twelve months of despair, from which I believe none of them ever fully recovered.

A card Lenny sent to his kids whilst he was on remand.

, daughter and son,

your lives' begun.

I've watched you both while you have grown.

Now woman and man, how time has flown.

You've both made me happy, never sad,

It makes me proud to be called your dad.

So please remember my love is true,

and I'll always be there, to see you

<u>through.</u>

179

Ronnie Knight.

A Tribute From
Ronnie Knight
GANGSTER AND LONDON 'FACE'

*When I first met Lenny, not I nor anyone could have guessed
what a powerful man he would grow up to be, because this was
back in the late fifties and the Guv'nor to be was about ten
years old – skinny, nervous and cowed.*

*At that time I was involved in the Longfirm game – you
know, where a business is set up, legit for a while until it
builds up a massive credit line, then bosh, move everything out
of the warehouse, flog it off cheap and start up somewhere else.
I had a bloke by the name of Jim McLean working for me. Big
fella, stood about six three and though I wouldn't go so far as
to say we were mates, we had the odd drink together and I
thought he was sound.*

*Anyway, I had some keys or something to collect from Jim,
so on the way up West I picked up my girlfriend Barbara and
called into his flat in Kent Street, Bethnal Green. This is when
I first clapped eyes on Lenny who I naturally assumed was
Jim's boy. Now, nothing to do with what I was to learn many
years later, but there was a definite atmosphere in that flat. Jim
lounged back in an armchair, full of himself as usual. But his
missus didn't seem comfortable. She brought tea in, but didn't
have one herself and she kept looking at Jim and looking away
as he looked up. The boy never opened his mouth, just stood
behind the settee – didn't sit on it – stood behind it against the
wall. And he kept looking at his dad same as his mum was
doing.*

Afterwards, when Babs and me were in the car, she said,

181

'They don't seem a very happy family. I felt sorry for that woman and the little boy.'

I don't know why I defended Jim because he was nothing to me and I'd sensed things weren't all that as well, but I wouldn't have it. 'Nah, Jim's alright, his missus and kid were probably a bit shy 'cos you were there.'

How can you work with someone for a couple of years, have a laugh and a joke and a lot of beers together and not realise that person is some sort of Jekyll and Hyde? Because that is exactly what that piece of shit, who called himself Jim McLean, turned out to be, and it was to be many years later that I learned the truth from Lenny himself.

Me and a few of the chaps used to go to boxing matches quite regular and every now and then we'd slip into an unlicensed fight. One night in particular one of the fighters on the card was under the wing of one of my mates so naturally I stuck my money on him to win. Did I make a mistake or what? Nobody told me he was up against this young fighter 'Mean Machine McLean'. Two minutes and it was all over and my bet was down the pan.

I never made the connection that this giant of a fella was anything to do with that frightened little boy I'd met years previous. And it wasn't until I was eventually introduced to Lenny and we struck up a friendship that I was put in the picture one night when we were discussing the old days and families.

By the time I found out what had been going on back then, Jim McLean was just a name from the past. But as long ago as it had been, the extent of his brutality to a family that wasn't even his own, still shocked and angered me.

182

For a start his real name was Jim Irwin, and he'd borrowed the McLean name when he married Lenny's widowed mum Rose. This in itself was an insult to the memory of a man Lenny swore to me was the best dad in the world. But worse than that, after a day's work in the warehouse or wherever, with all the usual joking and banter with me and the other chaps, he'd gone home to systematically beat, batter and abuse his wife and stepchildren.

I don't know anyone who doesn't hate this cowardly type of man and if only I'd known then what was going on behind closed doors, he would have paid a very heavy price. Believe me, in my world back then – it happened.

One small consolation that I have is the fact that I personally gave Jim a beating that left him on the floor. Unfortunately it wasn't payback for Lenny, but because he was making a nuisance of himself with a girl who not only worked for me but was a very good friend. All the details don't matter, but if I can use one of Lenny's sayings: 'You can't beat a good right hander.' That's exactly what knocked the fight out of Jim before he even knew what was going down.

I think the treatment he suffered as a child made Lenny into the unbeatable fighting machine that he became. But I've often wondered how he would've turned out without that terrible apprenticeship. I reckon he could've been a top businessman, because he was shrewd and had a sharp mind that never stopped turning. And that's what set him apart from most other people in the world where he made his living.

When I learned that Lenny was terminally ill I was totally gutted. And when he died that was made even worse by the fact that as I was banged up in prison and wasn't allowed out to pay my last respects to a man that gave respect to everyone. When his funeral was shown on the news, the television room was packed to the door with inmates and I tell you, you could've heard a pin drop. That was the sort of respect everyone had for him, even those fellas that had never met him.

Though violence was his business for most of his adult life, I can honestly say I never met a more friendly, warm and loyal man in all my life. The world lost a great character when he passed away and I don't care how big or tough they come, nobody in the future will ever be able to call themselves the Guv'nor without coming a poor second best to Lenny McLean.

A Tribute From
Mark Thornburrow
INMATE WITH LEN WHILE HE WAS AWAITING TRIAL

When I first met Lenny McLean I was on remand for murder and very, very frightened. I was eighteen. When he found out that I had stabbed another boy he really told me off for what I had done. Then he said if I was sorry for what I'd done, shaped myself up and took what was coming like a man, he would look after me. And he did. All the way through those terrible months he gave me the strength to face what was coming. He might have looked big and bad, but he was there for me like a father.

He said to me one day before I was sentenced, 'Look at it

A covert picture of Reg Kray that Lenny took when on a visit.

this way son. If they give you life at least you'll still be a young man when you've done your time. But I'm facing the same thing and if I get a rec of twenty-five at my age – I'm finished.

Lenny always thought of others before himself. He had a heart of gold and I owe him so much.

An Extract From

THE GUV'NOR by Lenny Mclean

It seems a lifetime since I first came through the gates of Brixton, and in many ways it was. In the last 12 months I've thought and thought more than I have ever done in my whole life. Can you imagine being on a murder charge, and I mean charge, not sentence, and you know you haven't committed the crime? You live and breathe it every second of the day. As you wake up in the morning, for one tiny second it's not there, but count to two and your head's filled. Murder-life-murder-life, and that goes on and on until you fall asleep, and even then it doesn't stop. It's terrible.

It's not the prison, it's the fucking charge. Three hours' sleep every night because your brain won't switch off and when it does, the dreams come. And then it's like being smothered or drowned. Everything presses down on you until you wake up. You can't breathe and one second later, murder-life-murder-life.

Can you, in your wildest dreams, imagine what Reg

Above: Lenny on his way to the Old Bailey for his murder trial.

Kray has been through? He went through a year just like me, but then he had the nightmare of facing 30 years behind the door. Thirty years — try and imagine it. It's the difference between a newborn baby and a settled married man. The difference between a Jack-the-lad at 35 and an old-age pensioner. You can't grasp it, can you? Nor can I.

Now think about Reg again. Could you be so strong? The media treat him like some exhibit in a cage. Whenever they're stuck for copy they stick another bit of shit in the papers. Do they say, 'Look at this man ... 30 years in prison and he's strong, fit and his mind's as sharp as it ever was.' Of course they don't, because those in power want him crucified. Why do I feel so strongly? Because I've known a tiny bit of what he's gone through, so I understand.

I'm using him as an example, and he's the best example. But now I understand people like Charlie Richardson, Tony Lambrianou, Joe Pyle, Charlie Kray, and many, many others, who've suffered and stayed strong.

The night before the verdict, I never even tried to close my eyes, and I'm not ashamed to say that in the middle of the night I got on my knees and prayed. I prayed for my own sake, but more than that, I prayed for Val and the kids. They'd suffered as much as I had, but in a different way, yet they never blamed me once for bringing all that aggravation to our home.

John and I had a cuddle downstairs, then we shook hands and I climbed the stairs surrounded by cozzers.

They weren't taking any chances on a bad result.

I mouthed a kiss towards Val as I stepped into the dock and she blew one back.

You could have heard a pin drop. I looked around the courtroom, then I studied the faces of the jurors one by one.

You — what do you know about my life? You look like you should be behind the counter of a bank. And the old girl with the glasses on, are you working out what to get your old man for his tea? The boy with the pimples, the girl who doesn't look older than my Kelly; who are you all? What are you thinking? Not one of them would let me catch their eye.

Reading through a bit of law bumph in my cell, I'd noticed that 'the defendant shall be judged by 12 of his peers'. Ray said that means equals, but don't make me fucking laugh. Look at them. Look at me. These little people, these straights whose only brush with the law was when they parked on a double yellow — they don't know anything about real life and they're getting ready to take mine away. They're going to bury me under concrete until I'm 69 years old

I looked away from them and glanced over to my Val but I couldn't stand the pain in her eyes, so I looked upwards to a little patch of blue-grey sky I could see through the rooflight.

I must have gone off somewhere in my head, because one minute I was thinking if that was how I would be seeing the sky for years to come, through glass, when all of a sudden I heard Judge Lowry say,

'What is your verdict?'

I just had time to say to myself, 'Please, God, help me for my family's sake,' and the foreman said, 'NOT GUILTY'.

I seemed to stand paralysed for ages staring ahead — then it sank in — 'NOT GUILTY'.

Those twelve ordinary people have suddenly gone from mugs to saints. They were on my side. They'd seen the truth and I loved every one of them.

The cake says 'Welcome Home Len...' He must have felt welcome indeed after twelve months inside on a murder rap.

I gripped the rail as a relief swept over me that I couldn't describe again if I tried. Then I couldn't help myself. I looked straight at Judge Lowry and burst into song.

'Always look on the bright side of life ... Da Da ... Da Da...'

He looked stern, then he smiled and said, 'Take that man down.'

As I walked down the stairs out of sight of the courtroom, I said to the two screws escorting me, 'Come on, boys, let's go down in style.' I pulled each of their caps round so the peaks were over their ears, linked arms with them, and as we reached the bottom of the stairs I started singing again. John was down one end of the passage and he was cheering and clapping; the three of us danced towards him, and I sang 'Always look on the bright side of life', then all the screws were clapping and patting me on the back. I thought of my Val, Jamie and Kelly and shouted as loud as I could, 'I'M GOING HOME!' – then I punched the air.

YES! THE GUV'NOR'S GOING HOME!

CHAPTER 6

Lenny The Actor

Knock someone out in the street and they give you five years. Do the same in front of a camera and they give you five grand.

IT WAS nothing more than natural progression that led Lenny to the acting game. He was a natural born showman who lived much of his life in high profile under the public gaze. He loved every minute of being in the limelight and why not? He'd put up with a hard and dangerous existence for most of his life so why shouldn't he reap the side benefits of his notoriety?

Everyone expected a show from Len, whether in the ring, on the cobbles or simply when listening to this larger-than-life humorous raconteur.

If Mike Reid hadn't suggested Lenny put himself up for a bit of film or TV work, someone else would have, because he was a natural. An outgoing, charismatic and very genuine personality and there are too few of these around anymore.

I don't know what was in his mind when he first put

Left: **Lenny at Pinewood Studios.**

195

himself up for a part, but I can guess. 'Piece of piss. Spout a few lines and walk away with the cash.' As he said, 'Knock somebody out in the street they give you five years. Do the same in front of a camera, they give you five grand.'

The reality came as a bit of a shock, as Paul Knight describes. For a start he'd never been a book reader. Now suddenly he had to study pages of script, take it in and understand the concept. Also he had to learn a certain amount of discipline when it was pointed out to him that the script had been sweated over and rewritten a hundred times before it was given to him, *'So please Lenny, don't re-work it to suit yourself!'*

Allowing that right from the start he was working with actors, who had been in the game for years, his performances by comparison were outstanding. Yet no matter which director he worked under, none of them ever got him to stick strictly to the script, but then again with his natural street talk he often put across a point better than some writer from another world.

When I first saw *Lock, Stock & Two Smoking Barrels* I laughed out loud when he referred to a young scouse villain as 'Short Stuff'. He'd obviously thrown this in during the scene because this phrase was Lenny's own and one I'd never heard used by anyone else.

With a couple of more years in front of the camera I truly believe that he would have gained enough experience for some foresighted producer to have him playing a major role in a series tailored to his unique presence. But it was never to be.

Barry the Baptist.

Lenny's final role – Barry the Baptist in *Lock, Stock & Two Smoking Barrels.*

Barry the Baptist

lock stock
& two smoking barrels

Above: Tony McMahon, pictured here between Lenny and Vinnie.

A Tribute From
Tony McMahon,
ACTOR

I was fifteen years old wen I first met Lenny. I was outside Camden Palace nightclub selling tickets and letting my friends through the fire exits. The rule was never get caught by Big Len – but of course we did!

After ducking and diving for a couple of years, Lenny took me under his wing and we formed a very strong relationship. Lenny was a very shrewd business man which opened many doors for me. He introduced me to the film world and many influential people. With his guidance I wound up to be one of London's top promoters.

I knew a side to Lenny that was practically unknown to others, a side of a man who was kind, gentle and a loving father who adored his wife and family.

When Val phoned to tell me of Lenny's illness, I went straight to the hospital. I looked into his eyes and said to myself, If anyone can be strong, it's this man I'm cuddling. From then on I went round to see Lenny and Val every day, and never left without a cuddle from the big man.

Even though Lenny may not be here to see me now, I know he's still there guiding and looking over me.

A Tribute From
Paul Knight,
TV PRODUCER

When we were casting for the 2nd series of the Customs and Excise drama The Knock, *Corinne Rodriguez my Casting Director introduced me to Lenny McLean who came up to audition for the part of Eddie Davies, an old time South London villain who was very heavily into bootlegging and protection. Lenny told us that he had been recommended to* the 'acting game', by his old pal the comedian Mike Reid of EastEnders *fame. Lenny was an extraordinary character – during the interview he did John Wayne and Jimmy Cagney impressions, cracked jokes and offered us all free entrance into the nightclubs he was currently minding. We were also offered roles in his life-story,* The Guv'nor, *a feature film to be made at Pinewood Studios in the near future.*

Lenny was perfect for the part of Eddie Davies, and although he had no acting training, was a natural. On his first day filming he arrived on set, accompanied as always by his minders, not realising the enormity of what he had got himself into. He was immediately surrounded by film technicians, lamps, cameras, make-up, wardrobe and all the paraphernalia of a film unit on location, a director who was up against the clock and all eyes and the camera focused exclusively on him. Lenny immediately forgot all his lines of dialogue and in desperation told the director he had learnt the wrong script. Lenny was not a man you argued with, and the director meeting him for the first time on that day was not inclined to. Hastily written cards with his dialogue were held in his eye-line and the script supervisor mouthed his lines to him. The result, when cut together, and although nerve-racking for the director, crew and most of all Lenny, was absolutely right. Lenny had tremendous presence, was totally believable and extremely charismatic. Over the weeks that followed he found out more about the process of film-making and gradually became more assured as an actor.

Right: **Paul Knight (standing), producer of** *The Knock,* **the show that gave Lenny his break.**

There was some opposition to his casting but his presence in the show, not just as the character Eddie Davies but as himself, was a talisman, as he was entertaining, always telling stories, forever the optimist and the enthusiast. At the end of the series the script called for him to be arrested by Customs and Excise in an enormous 'knock' when Customs raided his booze warehouse. We employed six stuntmen playing Customs Officers who hung on for dear life and were thrown effortlessly around the set during their attempt to arrest him. However, I decided to give him a short jail sentence so he could appear as Eddie Davies again in the third series which starred Dennis Waterman.

Over this period I was also producing London's Burning, *and Lenny would regularly pop into the studios in Bermondsey to update me on the progress of his film, which was always just weeks away from starting and gave me a copy of the manuscript of his autobiography* The Guv'nor *which I thought was brilliant and way above the normal run-of-the-mill ex-villain autobiographies. It captured the real Lenny, his background in Hoxton as a boy, his miserable childhood and the violent world that he inhabited, told in his own words, encapsulating his vivid recollections. Suddenly Lenny stopped coming to the studios and I didn't know right until the end that he had been taken ill.*

My most abiding memory of Lenny was after a press preview of The Knock *at a private cinema at Planet Hollywood in Leicester Square. A group of us, including Lenny, went for lunch in Soho and as we walked through the streets it was like a triumphal progress led by Lenny.*

Everybody knew him: doormen, bouncers, waiters, barrow boys, cabbies. They all called over to him, some to shake his hand, some to wish him luck.

It is incredibly sad that Lenny did not live to see the success of The Guv'nor *book and* Lock, Stock & Two Smoking Barrels *and I sincerely hope that his most prized ambition to make a film of his life story is fulfilled and that this film does justice to this extraordinary character.*

A Tribute From
Vinnie Jones
FOOTBALLER, ACTOR AND HARD MAN

Though I'd known about Lenny and his fearsome reputation for many years, it wasn't until we were both put up for parts in Lock Stock that we actually met at a pre-filming insurance medical. We had a good crack and a few laughs so by the time he turned up on set a month or so later I knew what to expect – a lot of the others didn't.

Though he was one of the nicest guys I've ever met he could turn on a terrifying appearance in a second – though thank God it was only for a laugh. We had lots of runners around the studio – young kids who'd go and get anything we needed. I can see Lenny now swelling himself up and roaring at one of these kids, 'OI YOU, OVER 'ERE NOW.'

Over came the youngster, literally shaking in his shoes and Lenny would change back into the bloke he really was

Two hard men together
– Lenny and Vinnie.

and say, 'Good boy, now giv'us a cuddle then go and get your Uncle Len a nice glass of lemonade.' He did that time and time again until they all got to know him.

Though he wasn't many years older than a lot of the people on the set, he was a father figure to everyone, myself included. He had a way about him that just commanded respect. Nothing to do with his size or reputation as a fighter but a special something I can't put into words. He never looked down on anybody and he didn't look up to anybody either, he accepted and gave respect to everyone no matter what job they were doing. And this respect was given back to him from the tea girls right up to the main players like Sting.

He didn't only do his own job well, his humour and enthusiasm was so infectious it brought out the best in everyone around him

Because our backgrounds were similar we spent a lot of time together between takes chatting about this and that. I think he was quite tickled by the fact that we both had hard men labels. More than once he said, 'Vinnie, how can this film go wrong? They've got the hardest fighter and the hardest footballer working together – what a team.' Something else he was always pushing at me until it became a sort of motto, was, 'Have respect for your opponents – respect for people that ain't as strong as you and have respect for the people you love.'

One of the saddest parts about Lenny's early death was that he wasn't able to make career mileage out of the movie's success. Most of us involved had done bits and pieces in front of the camera, but this was going to be the big one – and it was. I honestly think he could've gone anywhere in

209

the business after the performance he gave, because from the heart I've got to say that by anybody's standards he was the best actor that came out of it.

The last time I saw him was at the wrap party when the movie was completed. We all had a gut feeling that Lock Stock was going to be a winner and Lenny was as excited about the possibilities as all of us that had made it happen. He said to me, 'It's going to be a blinder, I reckon we're on the way up.' The next thing I heard was that this tough, genuinely honest and loveable character had passed away and I was totally gutted.

I feel sadness for his family and all the people that loved him, but also sadness for myself because I lost a good friend that day.

A Tribute From
Garry Bushell
JOURNALIST

Lenny McLean could have stepped right out of the pages of a Raymond Chandler novel. He was a big man, but not much wider than a beer truck, and he had a serious physical presence. When Lenny walked in a room you knew it.

When Lenny walked into my bar to film his appearance on my ITV show, Bushell On The Box, the producer turned so white he was almost see-through. It was like he had just sat up in the bath and spotted a piranha circling his *scrotum. The mere look of McLean was enough to intimidate the crew. My sound man, Neil, a karate black belt, admitted afterwards that he had spent the whole interview wondering whether he could have dropped the big man had Len thrown a strop. His conclusion was, 'Not an effing chance!'*

But naturally Lenny was a perfect gent. He respected my home, he was pleasant and polite, an entertaining guest, and he gave his time freely to the local tearaways who had rallied in my back garden. McLean had long been a legend to working class Londoners who considered him the Rocky Marciano of the unlicensed boxing world, and after the show he found himself mobbed by a small army of spotty teenagers.

Lenny's big bulldog face broke into an enormous grin. But he didn't bask in the glory and entertain them with gory tales of who he'd up-ended on the cobbles. The message he gave those kids was quite different. 'Shit up 'ere,' he boomed, poking a giant finger at his nose, 'Nut don't like it.' Over and over again: 'Shit up 'ere, nut don't like it.' In other words – cocaine mucks up your brain. I'd venture his little talk was a damn sight more effective than any lame government Just Say No poster campaign.

This was 1996, when Lenny was making a big impact as a villain in LWT's The Knock. *The acting came easy to him: he lived the part. But the batterings he'd endured hadn't deadened his brain.*

I first met Lenny in the eighties when he lived in East London, and knew that he had a mind as lively as those formidable fists. When Len recalled his legendary street brawls there was always a twinkle in his eye. He was funny.

Garry Bushell – one of Lenny's biggest fans.

Roy Shaw once swore blind that Lenny had only beaten him because he had taken Ginseng. Asked about Roy's claim, Lenny replied, 'Yes, it could have been the Ginseng he took... or it could have been the right-hander he took that put him in the third row.'

Priceless! Lenny McLean was as much a gent a he was a giant. It was a pleasure to have known him.

A Tribute From
Frank Harper
ACTOR

Before I took up acting full time I used to work in Smithfield meat market. I became mates with and worked alongside a fella by the name of John Wall and he introduced me to his cousin Lenny McLean. John, who himself died of cancer shortly before Len, had told me a lot about this big and very tough member of his family, so I was a bit unsure of what to expect from someone who called themselves a f.....g raving lunatic.

Instead of being the aggressive monster most people talked of, Lenny turned out to be the funniest man I ever met. No matter what problems I had or what pressure I was under, five minutes in his company would have me laughing. I have to say he was everything and more that made him one of the toughest I ever met, but that was his work and family and friends were given a completely different side of him.

As a put down to those people who said he was a bully

THE GUV'NOR – A TRIBUTE

who smashed up anyone who crossed him, there was a time when he caught a sixteen-year-old tearaway stealing the hubcaps from his car. Somebody had spotted this kid working his way through the cars parked behind the Camden Palace. They phoned the police then told Lenny, who was working on the door. He slipped quietly out of a back door and collared the youngster who by coincidence was just pulling off the last cap on Len's motor.

Did Lenny beat the living daylights out of him? No – He dragged him inside took him up to his office and made him sit at a desk and write out a hundred times, 'I must not nick Lenny's hubcaps – I must not nick Lenny's hubcaps'.

When the police eventually turned up Len kept them waiting outside his office until the boy had finished his lines, which by all accounts took a painful hour. If he'd had his way the law would never have been involved, but by this time it was out of his hands.

He was a strong man both mentally and physically who had a lasting impact on everyone who met him. All these people will remember him for many different reasons, but my own memories will be of his own special brand of humour and that belly laugh of his that was like a cannon going off.

Right: **Eddie Davies – at your service...**

A Tribute From
Eddie Jeffries,
BUSINESS ASSOCIATE AND FRIEND

This is a picture of Lenny and me just after being thrown off the set of one of the James Bond films at Pinewood Studios. Lenny, as usual, had all the actors and film crew laughing at his jokes – all except Cubby Broccoli, the producer!

Well what can you say about Lenny that hasn't already been said? That he was without question the toughest guy in Britain, and a one-man army. He was a true man amongst men and well respected by all who knew him. A good husband to his lovely wife Valerie and a good father to his son Jamie and daughter Kelly. And a true friend to me.

Wherever you are, Len, rest in peace and without pain.

God bless you.

Eddie

A Tribute From
Frank Buisson,
MINDER TO THE STARS

We came out of the same East End background, and have been pals since then. Len went his way and I went mine, but he always remained my role model and idol.

Right: Lenny and Eddie Jeffries by the James Bond studio.

If you challenged him, crossed him or he found you taking liberties with the weak and defenceless, then God help you. But you could never find a man with a bigger heart who went out of his way to help others.

Below: Len was no stranger to the stars. He is shown here with one of the biggest Starrs of them all – Freddie.

A Tribute From
Flanagan
FIRST-EVER PAGE 3 GIRL

I knew Lenny for 20 years. I thought of him as a giant of a man. People respected him in and out of the ring, but many people weren't lucky enough to know the two sides of the man. I was one of the lucky ones.

Women looked to Lenny as a sort of Galahad. They used to ask him many favours, and if someone had been unkind or threatening to them, a word from Lenny was enough.

He used to sit in a friend's shop in Roman Road and make us howl with laughter with stories of all the fights he'd had. People from all walks of life loved him, and he always told me how much he loved his Val and children.

Once I asked him, 'Lenny, of all the people who you've ever met, or admired, who is the top of your list?'

I expected someone rich and famous. He replied, 'Mother Theresa.'

That was our Lenny, our top man, our Galahad.

Lenny and Flanagan.

C H A P T E R   7

Lenny The Funeral

I can't and won't describe the tears and
fears of our private grief, but I can say
how I feel. Of course I don't want to die,
but I've accepted that that's the hand I've
been dealt and I'll deal with it in the same
way as I've faced every challenge in my life
– head on.

Lenny made his final journey in a blaze of publicity that would have gladdened his showman's heart. Every newspaper, even the up-market broadsheets, gave over a page to note the passing of the Guv'nor, while TV stations across Britain updated on the hour the progress of his funeral cortege. As we drove slowly through the East End with many in the crowd calling out 'God Bless Lenny' or 'Goodbye Len', I could hear that deep chuckle of his at every turn of the wheel.

At Ronnie Kray's funeral Lenny had said to me, 'Y'know what Peter? They can say what they like about East End people, but they don't half know how to give one of their own a proper send-off.' Unthinkable then, but as we followed Ronnie's horse-drawn carriage to Chingford Mount Cemetery I could not have imagined that the next time I would witness such a respectful spectacle would be at the funeral of my invincible friend who was sitting beside me.

As would be mirrored almost two-and-a-half years later for Lenny, when Ronnie's calvacade swept through the crowded streets, traffic and motorcycle police saluted the hearse as it passed. Lenny said, 'See that? I bet Ronnie's laughing his nuts off.'

As I saw it they were showing respect for the occasion – whereas in Lenny's case they were showing respect for the man himself. And why not? For over the years I'd noticed that 'Old Bill' were as eager to stop Len in the street and shake his hand, or call out from squad cars, just like any taxi driver would have. If the ordinary constable on the beat hadn't been so well disposed towards Len, I'm sure that at some point during thirty years behind the

226

wheel, they might have discovered he'd never held a driving licence. It was only at about age forty-six when he decided to 'Legal himself up a bit', that he thought it was about time he took a test – not surprisingly passing first time.

That day – 5th August 1998 – was one filled with many emotions. But overriding my great sense of loss was a greater sense of pride that this man I'd got to know so well could fill the streets of London with ordinary people, all wanting to pay affectionate tribute to the Guv'nor.

None of us could have known it that sad day, but this wasn't the end of Lenny McLean. It was the beginning of a growing interest in him that would take his name to every corner of Britain, and far beyond these shores. A legend in his lifetime – a legend for all time.

A Final Tribute
John Huntley's speech made at Lenny's funeral

Lenny. Well what can I say about Lenny that hasn't been said a million times? Fearless, bravest of the brave. The Guv'nor.

I'll start by saying how I first met Lenny. It was at Freddie Hill's gym. I was the only one in the gym when I heard a voice say, 'Freddie Hill about?'

I looked around and saw Lenny. He was about 28 at the time. I said, 'No, but he shouldn't be long.'

He was full of bounce, a right Jack the Lad. He said, 'Alright, I'll wait.' Then he whacked the speedball with a left hook which snapped it off the swirl and catapulted it across the gym. That speedball had been hanging there for ten years.

Vinnie Jones (centre) at Len's funeral.

Lenny had been in the gym for two minutes and was already being a nuisance. After that he would disrupt the gym every night, always larking about, but everyone loved him for it. Whenever the other fighters like Kevin Finnegan and Tony Sibson would come to the gym, the first thing they would say was, 'Where's Lenny?' The gym was never the same without him. The gym came alive when he walked in.

They say that you either have charisma or you don't. Lenny oozed it.

People used to think it was strange the way Lenny and I got on so well when our worlds were so far apart. Well, Lenny used to make people laugh. For example, how many times have you been in Lenny's company for more than five minutes and not ended up laughing at his East End wit and his one-liners. I think that is why we gelled so well.

Lenny used to say to me he never liked the business he was in. He did it to put, as he used to say, 'steam on the table'. He was in his element when he was holding court and having good people around him.

I will miss my old friend. Over the past twenty years I have been around Lenny through the good times and the bad. I won't talk about the bad times. But the good times, like his victories at the Rainbow, his first acting role, buying his lovely home in Kent and finally the publication of his book that has become a number one bestseller, and so many more, I have lost count of.

Then there is Val, Lenny's wife. Well, what can I say? If only all relationships were that successful. Lenny loved her to bits. When I look back on the days when I would call in to see Lenny for an hour and every ten minutes Lenny would ask Val, 'How about a nice cup of tea for me and John.' Now most wives would maybe make one or two cups and then say, 'No, I've already made two.' I was waiting for her to say this and in all those years she never did. She never moaned or complained, it was just done.

Lenny was so proud of his family. He used to say, 'My Val, she's my life. She's one in a million. My Kelly, she's proper. And Jamie, he's such a live wire.' He was so proud of them. And I know that they were proud of him. You know Lenny never feared anyone. The only thing that could beat him was something he couldn't see. How can you beat that? But he fought all the way with all his usual courage, right to the final bell.

Lenny said he wasn't afraid to die. I believe the thing that worried Lenny was not being able to see Val again. He just didn't want to leave her because he loved her so much. His family meant the whole world to him.

Lenny fought his way out of the East End backstreets to provide his family with a lovely house in Kent and made sure Val and the kids always had everything they ever wanted. That was always his main concern. He never asked for anything himself. As long as his family were happy, he was happy.

When Lenny arrives at the Pearly Gates, he will probably ask to be head doorman. But he won't have to tell anyone off this time around, just give them a cuddle.

This world seems so unfair. Just as everything was coming together after so many years for Lenny and then this happens. He had moved on to a different corner. He loved his acting and was just starting to enjoy life when it was so unjustly taken away.

The public only knew Lenny as the tough guy, the Guv'nor. But there was another side to Lenny that only his family and close friends knew. He had a much softer side.

There was one occasion amongst many others that I can remember. We were sitting in his back garden having a chat when we heard a loud clap. We looked up and someone had shot a bird out of a tree. The bird fell into someone's back garden in the distance. Lenny said to me, 'I can't believe that. What's the matter with people? That bird never hurt no one. What satisfaction could he have got by doing that?' To Lenny that was a true act of wickedness. He couldn't understand how anyone could be so heartless. He was looking at me for an answer. I didn't have one. I just said, 'We live in a crazy world, Len.' But that particular individual would probably be the first to point the finger at Lenny and say, 'There's the bad guy.'

In many ways Lenny was from another era. He was a one-

off, an old throwback to the likes of John Sullivan, Jack Dempsey and Victor McGlegan. He was the real life Rocky. He really was the last of the real tough guys.

There will never be another Lenny. He was a one-off. But I will never forget the Big Fella.

Thanks Lenny, for all the magical times that you let me share with you. Your life in many ways was like a roller coaster – full of ups and downs. But wasn't it exciting? Wasn't it just? I will miss you. Things will never be the same without you around.

Take care, my old friend. And as Lenny used to always say to me, just as I was leaving, 'Mind the road and don't talk to any strangers.' Thanks Lenny for being such a good friend. It was an honour to be yours.

God bless.

NIGHT I THREATENED TO GIVE RUBY SOME WHACKS

PART II OF KNOCKOUT STORY OF TV'S TOUGHEST MAN

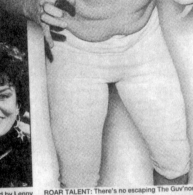

ROAR TALENT: There's no escaping The Guv'nor

KING of the toughs Lenny McLean showed TV loud-mouth Ruby Wax who was The Guv'nor—by threatening to put her over his knee and spank her.

Lenny—bootlegger Eddie Davies in TV's The Knock—recalled: "She was a b******. Before her chat show, she was timid and pleasant. In front of the camera she was like a man—big mouth and all aggressive."

But Lenny knew how to make her belt up. "In the break I said to her: 'Look here, pack it in with the lip or I'll pull you right over my knee in the middle of the show'.

'They should stick me in the Guinness Book of Records for being the first bloke to get Ruby Wax to shut her mouth!'"

Last week we revealed how Cockney giant Lenny, known as the hardest man in Britain, became a bare-knuckle boxing legend and then turned to acting.

Now he has put his amazing life story on record in his book The Guv'nor, up to the one fight he knows he can't win. For Lenny is dying of lung cancer.

When Lenny, 49, started out he was more at home fighting thug with his fists than rubbing shoulders with stars.

But he soon found it could be good for business. Lenny recalls: "Jerry O'Dowd asked if I'd step in between his brother Boy George and some slags who were giving him grief.

"I can't say George is my cup of tea, but he was polite and showed me respect, so I squared his problem."

Lenny said there was more to being The Guv'nor than bashing people. It took over his whole life. He revealed:

❝ You can't pick and choose. Whatever comes up has to be faced, no matter how bad or dangerous.

If somebody's in trouble, they think of Lenny.

They know that once I've taken their problems on board, it isn't a problem for them anymore.

ONE of the funniest men I've ever met was Freddie Starr, who had a bit of trouble he wanted sorted out. I agreed to meet him at his club near Windsor, with my pal Johnny Nash.

But Freddie's not there. Eleven, 12, one o'clock, and I'm getting the right hump. Half past one. Bang, the door opens and in walks Freddie Starr.

He's got both hands over his eyes and says: 'I'm so sorry I'm late. I ain't had a wink of sleep. I've been up all night with a bird.'

Then he lets his hands go and two big bloodshot eyes come shooting out on the ends of springs. Me and John fell about. How can you tell off a geezer like that?

We settled down and I asked him what the problem was. Turns out it was hardly a problem at all—or I should say to me it looked like nothing.

One phone call, and two minutes later it was all squared. Fred was well chuffed.

Sometimes, like in Fred's case, all I

STARR MATE: Lenny's book tells how he sorted out a problem for Freddie

EXCLUSIVE
By MIKE RIDLEY

have to do is growl over the phone or not even get involved—just let my name be put up. ❞

Lenny, of Bexleyheath, Kent, revealed how movie producers wanted to make a film about his life.

There was only one actor he wanted for the star role—Craig Fairbrass, from London's Burning. He soon found himself in the heat of real-life action with The Guv'nor.

But first Lenny took him to Pinewood for the auditions. Ray Winstone was there, so was Glen Murphy—a bit of a boxer who looked good.

Lenny said:

❝ At the time Craig didn't have a big name so I shoved him to the front where he would be seen. The producer clocked him and says: 'That's Lenny McLean'.

There's loads of money in the film game once it's at the box office, but until then you don't get a tanner.

I was still ducking and diving, taking on minding and working at a club. One night Craig and an actor

pal of his, Dave, came down to the club and got an idea of what it's like for me being The Guv'nor.

As we're talking, two big drunks barge their way through, shoving us out of the way—no excuse me, nothing.

One of these mugs says to his mate: 'Look up, it's McLean—The ****ing Guv'nor'. He goes to throw a right hander.

One left hook, one right and they're on the deck. ❞

WE went upstairs to the restaurant and we've only just sat down when in walks the actor Denzel Washington.

He's all excited and says, 'There's an ambulance downstairs and the police'. I said: 'Oh yeah, someone must have got run over'. ❞

Sadly the film ran into finance problems and was never made.

But Craig still made the breakthrough into movies when Sylvester Stallone chose him out of thousands to work in Cliffhanger.

Lenny said: "Always looking out for our film, Craig slipped the script to Stallone, who reckoned that Lenny McLean was like a real-life Rocky and that he'd like to meet me. That's some gee." Lenny had up to

3,000 unlicensed no-holds-barred fights—and won all of them.

He also helped launch millionaire boxing promoter Frank Warren—his nephew.

Lenny said: "He started out in the fight game putting up posters and organising venues for me and went on to become a force to be reckoned with.

"He's grafted well and used his nut all the way."

NOW, as Lenny looks back on a life packed with action, it's not the moments of violence or victory that he treasures.

He says: "You might get the impression that I get up in the morning and fight people until I go to bed.

"What you don't know is the good parts that make my life worthwhile. My two smashing kids, Kelly and Jamie, growing up, their first steps. Taking them to the zoo, teaching them to ride a bike.

"And, of course, there's Val. The older we get, the closer we become.

"We like going to shows or out to dinner with good people. Or just watching telly and having a cuddle.

"It's miles away from how I brought bread into the house.

"I lived in two worlds, one from choice, the other by necessity. It was all I knew.

"But for any kid reading this who thinks my lifestyle exciting enough to be worth copying—think again.

"Society's different now. Get yourself a decent education, aim high and have respect for people—because it's the only way to get on today."

© Lenny McLean and Peter Gerrard. Extracted from The Guv'nor by Lenny McLean with Peter Gerrard, Blake Publishing, £14.99.

To order a copy of The Guv'nor ring 0171 381 0666.

NO CONTEST: Ruby Wax was silenced by Lenny

CHAPTER 8

Lenny The Legacy

I've lived a dangerous life and could have died a hundred times over. But even when I faced guns and knives, or the blood was pouring out of me, I never considered the possibility that my days might be numbered. When you're my age and you go to funeral after funeral it makes you realise our time in this world is limited. It didn't worry me too much, just firmed up my conviction that you have to live every day to the full – do what you have to do and never have regrets because, believe me, you never know what's around the corner.

MEET the hardest bloke in Britain: Actor/author LENNY McLEAN.

Veteran of hundreds of unlicensed fights, shot twice, 20 years as a bouncer, time 'inside', survived a 'couple of stabbings'. Lenny, 49, gave up the fight game to star in TV's The Knock and new movie Lock Stock And Two Smoking Barrels. And now he's facing the biggest fight of his life — against cancer. Lenny spoke to ALLY ROSS, who agreed with every word . . .

Wandsworth jail . . . had brush with McLean

Lenny, we know you're a big softy at heart, tell us about the pub where you met your wife Valerie. "You're right *(Thank God!)* I am romantic. I walked into the Royal Standard in Hackney 31 years ago and saw this beautiful woman. Thirty years we've been together and I have put her through hell yet we're still together. She's my life.

"We try and go back to the Royal Standard during the week, people there treat me well and leave me alone. Beautiful."

What about wining and dining? "Two places. I love going for a Chinese at The Lotus in Docklands, or Propaganda in Great Eastern Street for a prawn cocktail. That puts a smile on my face. I don't let anyone interfere with me

Pub treated Len like a Royal

WITH HARD MAN LENNY McLEAN

but I'm not in the fight game anymore. Anybody who wants to have a go I just swerve them completely.

"People still want to talk to me about violence but that's all in the past."

Phew. You've worked some of the toughest clubs as a bouncer. Which was hardest? "At one old London club I took on 18 lads who refused to pay for drinks. I dealt with nine and the others ran away — shortly after that I was shot. Toughest of the lot was Glasgow's Tuxedo Princess — hardest in London was Camden Palace. But I'm glad to be out of it. I couldn't handle the kids nowadays."

Hard day's night . . . Camden Palace

What was the worst prison, Brixton? "Nah Wandsworth. They had me locked in my cell all the time, awful."

Where do you find happiness now? "I'm an East End boy but paradise is my home in Bexleyheath, Kent, with my wife and kids. I'm out in the country and sometimes think I've already died and gone to heaven, surrounded by angels.

"It's hard for me, I've accepted I've got cancer. But I'm going to fight all the way."

●Lenny's life story The Guv'nor is out now, published by Blake.

Prawn brokers . . . the Propaganda bar

EVEN NOW, after his death, Lenny's story continues to move and affect ordinary people, not only in this country but around the world. The following pages display how Lenny, the kid from Hoxton, was catapulted to fame; and show the fondness with which his name will be remembered.

I'M THE HARDEST MAN IN BRITAIN, I CAN'T BELIEVE CANCER'S GOT ME

Hard act . . . Lenny first realised s

By JOHN ASKILL

BRITAIN'S hardest man Lenny McLean spoke last night of his desperate fight against cancer and said: "I still can't believe it has got me."

Fearsome Lenny, who battered scores of opponents into submission as a bare-knuckle brawler, said: "I have always felt nothing could beat me — certainly no man ever has.

"I have been in some tough scraps and all my aggression will now be channelled into battling within.

"I know this will beat me but I'll fight all the way. At the end I'll sing my theme song — Always Look on the Bright Side of Life."

The 6ft 3in Cockney giant — known to fans of TV Customs thriller The Knock as bootlegging villain Eddie Davies — told how he first realised the disease had a grip on him.

Despite his massive muscles and superb fitness he suddenly found he had no breath to climb **STAIRS** on a movie set — or any strength to lift a **SUITCASE** on holiday.

I still felt so fit and strong inside me

Doctors have put him on a gruelling course of radiotherapy but have told him he will probably not survive past the end of the year.

Lenny, 49, said: "I've been for the X-rays and for the scans and it doesn't look good. I'm absolutely devastated and so is my family.

"I can't believe it — I still felt so fit and strong. Until a few weeks ago I was still running four miles a day and working out three or four times a week in the gym.

"But I suppose it is the cigarettes that have got me. I used to roll m own from loose tobacco. I'd hav five or six or even seven a day

"I can't believe how quickly has hit me. I have already lost fou stone in six weeks."

Last night Lenny, wife Val, 4 and children Jamie, 26, and Kell 25, were trying to come to ter with their heartbreak.

The 20st giant, originally fro Bow, East London, turned to actin after years as a streetfighting kin He had earned an awesome reput ation in bare-knuckle bouts befo becoming a minder and bounce

He was shot twice, knifed tw and even acquitted of murd serving 18 months for GBH.

His showbiz career was launch by Cockney comic and EastEnd

ls of his toughest scrap of all

...g during the making of a film with soccer tough guy Vinnie Jones

Pals . . . hug from EastEnders' Martine McCutcheon

Knocking around . . . with telly co-star Ian Burfield

Devoted family . . . Lenny with Val, Jamie and Kelly

...ho told him: "You just be yourself."
...making a movie Sting and soccer Jones that Lenny ...ing was wrong.
...n — called Lock, ...moking Barrels — ...the top of an old ...th London.

...ed to read ...a breather

...here were five or ...irs and everyone ...could not get my ...o stop for a rest ...ch flight, just to

...ers I pretended I ...to read through ...minute — but I ...self.
...art was churning

away. At the end of filming the cast and crew organised a football match. I asked Sting to put me in goal and said to Vinnie Jones, 'For God's sake don't pass me the ball Vinnie — I can't breathe'.
"I knew there was something very wrong but I had no idea it was cancer.
"After the warehouse problem Val decided I needed a holiday and we flew to Spain thinking the sunshine would sort me out.
"I had got some antibiotics from my doctor and expected to be straight back to normal.
"But when we got to Spain I couldn't even carry the suitcases to our chalet. It was that quick.
"When we got home, Val rang the doctor's. We didn't think it was serious but it was unusual for me to be ill at all."
Within days Lenny was lying in Queen Mary's Hospital in Sidcup, Kent, not far from the family home

in Bexleyheath. A woman doctor gently broke the news that tests had shown terminal cancer of the lungs and brain.
Lenny said: "I said to her, 'Will you tell me how long I've got?' She didn't answer so I asked outright, 'Do I have a year?'
"She looked me straight in the eye and said, 'Six months to a year — but you have got to fight'.

I kept thinking the doctor must be wrong

"Even as the doctor was telling me, I still wasn't frightened — I just felt hurt. I kept thinking. 'You're wrong. I can't be ill. ⅓ still look the same. I still feel the same, apart from a cough'.
"My wife and kids were there. We were all at the hospital together, trying to take it all in. We were all shocked and upset." Bat-

tler Lenny has come a long way since he made it his ambition to be the best fighter in junior school.
His showbiz career has brought him into contact with a host of stars including EastEnders' Martine McCutcheon, Hollywood idol Bruce Willis, comic Freddie Starr and ex-Minder favourite Dennis Waterman.
He made ten episodes of ITV's The Knock before landing the role in black comedy Lock, Stock and Two Smoking Barrels.
He added: "The film comes out in September and I also have a fighting video and a book about my life coming out.
"In the meantime I want to make things last. I want to see Christmas and I want to spend as much time as I can with my wife and kids.
"This is it, the big one, the fight of my life. The message to all the people who know me is simply this: I'll fight the only way I know how — and that's head on."

The Guv'nor dies in his sleep after long battle with cancer

The big fight is over for hardman Lenny

STORY BY ANDREW BARROW

THE GUV'NOR, Lenny McLean, has lost his long battle against lung cancer.

The Bethnal Green street-fighter, who earned his reputation as Britain's hardest man with 3,000 undefeated bare knuckle fights, died in his sleep on Tuesday morning.

His family - wife Valerie, son Jamie and daughter Kelly, were with him when he died. He was 49.

The 6ft 3in man-mountain, from Strahan Road, was diagnosed with lung and brain tumours this Spring.

In typical Lenny style, he vowed to fight the disease "the only way I know how - and that's head on."

Peter Gerrard, co-author of Lenny's autobiography, The Guv'nor, said: "This was Lenny's toughest scrap of all.

PRIVILEGED

"But despite immense bravery it was one he couldn't win."

"When you asked him how he was it was always 'top of the world, strong as a bull', right up until the end.

"I feel privileged to have been close to him and will never forget his humour and his big heart."

Lenny's wife, Valerie, said: "All his life, Lenny's only concern was for me, Jamie and Kelly.

"His life was full of violence but he never brought any of that home.

"He was so big and strong I thought he would go on forever but when the end came he faced it like the proper man he was.

"He knew we were with him when he died, so he was surrounded by love.

Tributes are pouring in for Lenny from the East End's famous faces.

LEGEND

Close friend, Charlie Kray, said: "Another legend has gone from the East End, God bless him and may he rest in peace."

East End actress, Helen Keating, said: "I'm so sorry he died before he saw his dream come true, he so wanted his book to become a film.

"Its going to be a duller place without him

Former Kray henchman, Tony Lambrianou, said: "He was a hard man but he was a fair man as well.

"Just when things were working out for him this happened."

■ Lenny McLean and wife Val who nursed him through his last illness

■ LENNY'S autobiography The Guv'nor has shot to the top of The Times book chart.

His story, from a Bethnal Green youngster to the Guv'nor of East London, was documented in last week's Advertiser.

Despite his illness, he was determined to promote the book. He was due to appear at a book signing at Liverpool Street Station WH Smith's on the day he died.

Co-author Peter Gerrard said: "Lenny knew, by the way the book was selling, that his story was a good one."

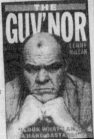

"LOOK WHAT I AM... A HARD BASTARD"

Lenny's funeral

Lenny's funeral is expected to be the biggest in the East End since Ron Kray's in 1995.

A horse-drawn hearse will lead the cortege through Hoxton, Bethnal Green and Roman Road next Wednesday before arriving at the City of London Crematorium, Aldersbrook Road, Manor Park, at 2pm.

The funeral cortege will leave Lenny's Bexley Heath home at 12 noon.

THE GUV'NOR

LENNY McLEAN

LOOK WHAT A HARD BASTARD

Death claims the king of the bare knuckle fighters, but his story has already sold out its first print run. **Dan Glaister** reports

Legend of Lenny lives on – as a bestseller

LENNY McLean, one of the most successful bare-knuckle fighters in Britain, has died of brain and lung cancer at the age of 49.

But the larger-than-life East End figure, who never lost one of his 3,000 fights, will embroider his legend when his autobiography tops the bestseller lists this weekend.

The Guv'nor, not officially published until Saturday although it is already on sale in some bookshops, has sold out its first print run of 10,000 copies in the three weeks since it became available. With a second run of 100,000 ordered, it could become one of the biggest-selling sporting books ever, according to its publisher.

McLean will come even more into the public eye with the release of the film Lock, Stock And Two Smoking Barrels, in which McLean has a starring role as a hardman called Barry the Baptist.

There is also talk of a film being made of his life story and even of a computer game about him. Last year he appeared in the film The Fifth Element, starring Bruce Willis.

Yesterday the publishers of The Guv'nor and the book's co-author were unsure whether to celebrate or mourn.

Crime writer Peter Gerrard, who wrote the book with McLean, said: "I have very mixed emotions. The book was turned down on many occasions and now with going to the top of the best-

seller lists, we've won. I'm so pleased for Lenny. He was both brawn and brain. He was very shrewd and very businesslike, which often fooled people."

McLean last hit the headlines in 1992, when he was tried for a murder at a nightclub where he worked as a bouncer. He was acquitted on the murder charge, but served 18 months in jail for grievous bodily harm.

But it was as bare-knuckle fighter and a figure involved in the more marginal sides of East End life that McLean was known. For Ronnie Kray, whose funeral McLean attended, he was "one of the best people I have ever met . . . a gentleman and one of the best fighters I have ever seen."

Reggie Kray called him "a legend in his own lifetime", while the last of the trinity, Charlie Kray, declared: "I have the greatest respect for him as a fighter. I have an even greater respect for him as a man."

McLean was known throughout London for 20 years as a boxer and a bouncer, and was a big draw on south London's unlicensed fighting scene. He was featured on News At Ten attacking another fighter known as Brian "The Mad Gypsy" Bradshaw after he headbutted McLean before the beginning of a fight. In one arranged fight in the 1970s, McLean was flown to New York by the Mafia to take on their leading bare-knuckle fighter, John McCormack, in a multi-million dollar bout. McCormack

lasted less than three minutes.

McLean was also brought in to intimidate an IRA-backed gang in London involved in a money-laundering scam.

Gerrard explained that when he met McLean, shortly after the fighter had served his prison term, they agreed to collaborate on a book. "Reggie Kray sent me along to meet him. We hit it off on that first night. His prison term made him rethink his whole life."

The book was commissioned and then rejected by a

publisher before it was picked up by Blake Publishing. The advance to the pair was £1,000. "It's like a wonderful weepy film," said publisher John Blake. "He's finally persuaded a publisher to put out his book and he's been proved right. Yet again he's come out on top.

"It's extraordinary timing that he has died. It's very bizarre. I don't think he would have been bitter. The attention would have pleased him enormously. He will be looking down from heaven and laughing."

McLean was taken ill four

months ago while on holiday in Spain. On his return he thought he was suffering from the effects of flu and decided to "work off" the symptoms, running an extra mile every day. After this failed he was diagnosed as having lung and brain cancer.

Two weeks ago he attended a book signing at an Oxford Street bookstore, but died on Tuesday.

"He hung on for the signing," said Gerrard. "After that he went downhill. But the signing was such a success that he kept saying, 'We've got a bestseller.' Of

course, we had to agree with him."

In Lock, Stock And Two Smoking Barrels, McLean appears alongside another hard man, Vinnie Jones. They were two tough guys together," said Gerrard, "although I wouldn't say Vinnie was in the same league as Lenny."

Yesterday, the footballer paid tribute to the fighter turned-actor. "Lenny was like an uncle to me and to every one on the set of Lock Stock. He taught me the ropes and will be sorely missed. A natural character."

Lenny McLean, alias The Guv'nor . . . he took part in 3,000 bare-knuckle fights and never lost one

LENNY MCLEAN

The former bare-knuckle fighter on boxing beef, taping slashed throats and Freddie Starr

As an unspeakably tough streetfighter and club bouncer, your reputation as "The Guv'nor" has been well earned over a period spanning more than 2,000 fights. Have you ever made a grown man cry just by looking at him?

No, but I've made grown men very frightened on many occasions. I like to think it's through them taking a liberty and knowing they're in the wrong. Sometimes just a growl is enough to sort someone out. As I get older, I don't want to hit you on the chin – I can't be fucking around with that – so if a growl can do it, and I can get rid of you that way, I'd sooner do that.

What's the biggest purse you've won in a bare-knuckle fight?

I had a fight with a guy 20 years ago and got £36,000. It was an unlicensed fight: all-in, anything goes. Where else could I get that money for a day's work? Trouble is, you spend it easy when you're young – you knock the tank out because you think it's never gonna end. It's only when you get a bit older and wiser you realise you've been getting fucked along the way.

Did you ever take on any overseas champions?

I once went to New York to take on the Mafia's best man. He was the hardest bloke I ever fought – big black fella, six foot eight, hugely powerful guy, 24 stone. I got four rib-breakers into him, jumped back and kicked him as hard as I could in the balls. I got one to his kidneys and he went down, and as he's getting up I kicked him full in the face. Six punches to the jaw, cheek and forehead finished him. He only lasted two-and-a-half minutes. All I could think about was getting my hands on that money. They put me up in the Plaza Hotel and when we got back from the fight, I said to my mate, "We've been paid, now let's go. I don't think we'd better wait here in case they want to blow our heads off." We went to the airport and waited there for ten hours for the flight.

Why didn't you ever turn pro?

When I was a young kid I was a bit wild, and I wouldn't have anybody tell me what to do. I just wanted the money, and I wasn't the kind of guy who'd train six or seven weeks for a fight. Couple of grand and I'd fight the next day.

Have you ever bitten off an ear, Tyson-style?

Yes, well, not an ear – but I bit a bloke's throat in a fight about 20 years ago, broke his jaw in seven places. He was actually a friend of mine – and thank God they managed to save his life. That's why I don't drink now: not Christmas, not birthdays – never. I think drink is the root of all evil. If I'd had booze and you were sat there and you were an enemy of mine, I'd be planning how to hurt you,

and that's wrong. Then again, you shouldn't be in my company if you're my enemy.

Are there really no rules in bare-knuckle fights?

It's up to you. How do you want it? Do you want a "straightener" – which has a few rules – or do you want to go "all-in?" Biting? Kicking? No problem, you can do anything, as long as you agree. If we're fighting for £20K and it's winner take all, anything goes – hammers, the lot.

Did you ever train for a fight by punching strung-up sides of beef, like Sly did in *Rocky*?

Strangely enough, yes. I used to run five miles a day, then go to this place where a mate of mine worked and have a go at the beef. Really smash 'em up, hurt my hands and everything. It's a fucking hard way to train, but at the same time, where are you going to get anything better at five in the morning? I got on that kick after seeing *Rocky*, as it happens. Stallone: he once sent me a letter when I was in prison, telling me not to give up. Respect.

Who was the weediest opponent you ever fought in a bare-knuckle fight?

No one, really. When people are putting their money down, they don't want to throw it away on some muppet. There was a gypsy from Doncaster and he wasn't too clever, but he might have been okay in his circle. I had him.

Have you ever come to the rescue of any famous people?

Yeah, many a time, as long as those people were in order and they had a genuine grievance. If they hadn't, I wouldn't have come to their rescue. I helped Boy George when someone was giving him grief. And Freddie Starr had a problem one day, so I met up with him, made a few calls and nipped it in the bud. No big deal.

Do you think the streets would be a safer place if the public turned vigilante?

Go back to the Sixties and yes, maybe. People like the Krays, the Nashes and other families had a lot of respect. Things could be controlled by a wave of a finger or a flash of a gun. These days, kids don't give a fuck. They're madmen, drugs everywhere and they'll blow you away. There's less respect now than there's ever been. Trouble is, sometimes you end up in bother when you try to help people out. One time this bloke's walking past a club I'm minding, and he's nutted a couple of old people, so I said, "I gotta hurt him." I gave it to the guy, took his pants off, smashed him up and slung him out the back. Cozzers only tried to nick me.

What's the worst injury you've ever suffered?

I've been shot twice – once up the arse. I got stabbed in the leg, too. I just left it, and it went a bit off and I nearly lost my leg through gangrene. I had about six operations, and luckily

they saved it. The worst injury I ever saw was someone get his throat cut in a club I was working at. There was blood everywhere. We held his neck together with tape.

You spent a year in jail awaiting trial on a murder charge which you were cleared of. What privileges did your reputation earn you?

The screws gave me a wide berth: plenty of room, which suited me and them. I had all-afternoon visits – and no one gets all-afternoon visits – plus loads of tobacco. In the nick, there's always someone who wants help, and one time it was this doctor who worked there. I helped him out and I got him to get me a mobile phone. Lovely.

Is it true that most hard people were physically beaten as kids?

Oh my good God, yes. My childhood was terrible. I had a fucking dreadful stepfather, used to beat me all the time. I don't like stepfathers, because they never love the children like their own. In my case, he was violent and brutal, and he put me through hell. The only good thing that's come out of my stepfather being a bully is that I've grown up to be a proper man, and if you're in trouble, I'll fucking die with you.

When did you realise your talent for fighting?

When I was a young kid at school. If you were the best fighter, you were like a celebrity. You were looked up to. But as you get older, being the tough guy becomes a fucking headache. I want people to like me 'cos I'm a nice guy, not 'cos I'm mad or a lunatic.

You recently turned your hand to acting, and had a part in the TV series *The Knock*. Did you do any telly work before that?

I did some BT adverts – I was a boxer in one – but some fucking dog phoned BT and told 'em I'd been on a murder charge and they edged me out. *The Knock* was fantastic. Done me proud. And I just done a film with Vinnie Jones, called *Lock, Stock And Two Smoking Barrels*.

Which celebrity would you like to take on?

Arnold Schwarzenegger – he's just an actor that's had a lot of luck. I'd take him in about six seconds. Stallone – four seconds; it'd take me that long to get hold of him, he's so little. Bruce Willis – couple of seconds. I'd get 'em all in a room and strangle the lot of 'em. No problem.

Bloody hell. Are you indestructible, then?

Well, I'm dying now – I've got cancer. I've got to fight it, but it's gonna be the hardest fight I've ever had in my whole life. It gives you a good challenge. Nothing worries you any more. I'm focused. When you've had a death sentence, it's the only thing on your mind. **FHM**

Interview by Mike Peake. The Guv'nor is out now from Blake Publishing, priced £14.99.

TIM O'SULLIVAN/KATZ

THE EAST END BIDS GO
LAST ROU

Lenny's coffin is taken to the hearse

Tribute in flowers to The Guv'nor

A touching message from wife Val

In memory of Daddy Cool

Advertiser SPECIAL

BY ANDREW BARROW

EAST Enders turned out in force yesterday (Wednesday) for the funeral of the Guv'nor, Lenny McLean, who died last week.

In the biggest funeral since Ron Kray's in March 1995, thousands of East Enders lined the streets and hung from upper floor windows to catch a glimpse of the cortege as it gave the bare knuckle fighting legend one last tour around his beloved East End.

The horse drawn carriage, along with two hearses just for flowers, travelled through Hoxton and down Bethnal Green Road and Roman Road towards the City of London Crematorium.

Lenny's son Jamie commented on the reception his father's trip was getting.

SHOWMAN

He said: "He was a real showman, my dad, he'd have loved all this."

The hearse travelled from Lenny's Bexleyheath home to Hayes and English funeral directors in Hoxton Street.

Lenny's oak coffin with gold handles was transferred to the Victorian glass-sided carriage pulled by four black-plumed horses.

The carriage pulled away through Hoxton, through the East End, and on to the City of London Cemetery in Manor Park, the resting place of Lenny's father.

VINNIE

<u>Mourners included East End faces such as former Kray henchman, Tony Lambrianou, and minder, Dave Courtney.</u>

Famous faces included football hardman, Vinnie Jones, who stars alongside Lenny in the feature film, Lock, Stock and Two Smoking Barrels and

Mourner: Vinn Jones

Charlie Kray sent

London brass, film ab

The Rev M co-auth rard.

Mour the bac watche from o

Flow sages f league author,

Rom McQue the nig of bou Guv'n

Tribu

East Enders in crowded Hoxton Street as the c

orsedrawn hearse passes a hoarding advertising his new film, Lock, Stock And 2 Smoking Barrels

Deepest
mpathy
BLESS
NNIE & Family
KING OF
OU TODAY
E KRAY

his prison cell

raig Fair-
v Lenny in a
uv'nor.
ed by the
culogy by
, Peter Ger-

ive deep at
e others
eedings

luded mes-
and col-
Kray and

le
hroughout
hundreds"
o The

as of Lon-

don and even from Lenny's friends in Glasgow.

Lenny was felled last week by lung and brain cancer.

On the same day, it was announced that his autobiography, The Guv'nor, had fought it's way to number one in the book charts.

On hearing of Lenny's death, co-author, Peter Gerrard, said the popularity of the book was nothing Lenny didn't already know.

MOTHER TERESA

He said: "Lenny knew, by the way the book was selling, that his story was a good one."

When his illness was diagnosed in the spring, doctors gave Lenny no chance of survival but he vowed to promote the book come what may

and was due at a signing session at Liverpool Street Station the day he died.

East End actress and friend of Lenny, Helen Keating, said Lenny's one wish was to have the film of his life made.

She added: "I'm so sorry he died before we had the chance to even begin making the film.

Britain's first topless Page 3 girl, Flanagan, said: "I once asked Lenny who he most admired.

"With all the people, the villains and the stars he has met I thought it would be someone rich or famous.

"Immediately he came back with 'Mother Teresa' which shows the side to Lenny that made him such a great guy to know."

Mourner: Tony Lambrianou

The Guvnor – Lenny McLean (Blake Publishing, £14.99)

Until his recent, untimely death, Lenny McLean was known throughout the East End of London as the "Guvnor", and it's this label that gives us the title for his chart-topping autobiography.

Lenny McLean came from humble beginnings to become one of the most feared men in Britain, if not the world.

Born in Hoxton, London, to a large but loving family, things started to go wrong when his father died very young.

The subsequent abuse he received from his stepfather helped mould the man whose reputation always went before him.

Often tragic, often very funny, the Guvnor tells the story of a sometimes brutal but mainly kind, generous and loving man whose reputation as the Guvnor was only relevant on the streets and not where he was most happy, at home with his wife and kids.

DYLAN THORLEY

LENNY'S BOOK No1 HIT

STREETFIGHTER Lenny McLean lost his toughest battle as his life story rocketed to number one in the book charts.

Lenny, 49, died of cancer on Tuesday as thousands bought his autobiography after it was serialised by the News of the World.

The book The Guv'nor, by Lenny McLean with Peter Gerrard, sold 25,000 copies in its first week. Publishers Blake ordered a second print run of 100,000. It was the third time in two months that books featured in this paper sold out in a week.

The £14.99 book, telling of Lenny's 3,000 bare knuckle fights, can be ordered on 0171 381 0666.

Courageous Lenny died with his wife Valerie, 47, and their children Jamie, 26, and Kelly, 25, beside him at home in Bexleyheath, Kent.

Knuckle power . . . A mourner with a handle on finery waits for Lenny McLean's cortege, which left the Hoxton funeral parlour, fronted by friends' wre

East End farewell for bare

Duncan Campbell at the funeral of a best-selling 'character'

LENNY McLean's book may have just made it into the best-seller lists but the final chapter was completed in east London yesterday, and rather earlier than planned. Britain's best-known bare knuckle fighter, was given an East End send-off as traditional as the pie and mash shop next door to the Hoxton funeral parlour which held his coffin.

He had died of cancer, aged 49, just as his autobiography, The Guv'nor, had become a best-seller, and just three weeks before the film in which he stars, Lock, Stock and Two Smoking Barrels, opens in London. As he put it himself in the book's epilogue, "one minute I'm looking years ahead — then bosh, it's all over."

The funeral procession set off from McLean's old stamping ground of Hoxton, in east London where a mixture of elegantly suited gangland and clubland members had gathered to say their farewells. Four horses, with plumes as dark as the reputations of some of the faces lining the old market street, drew the coffin round the corner from 61 Gopsall Street where he had been born in his grandmother's bed in 1949.

McLean had made his name as an unlicensed fighter with what he claimed were more than 2,000 victories — "some in the ring, many on the cobbles and many more in the pubs and clubs I've minded over 20 years". He had fought for purses as high as £60,000, on both sides of the Atlantic.

Recently, he had also faced a less welcome spotlight when charged and acquitted at the Old Bailey of the murder of a

McLean's funeral cortege passing through the East End today

Guv'nor gets an East End send-off

In his heyday: The imposing figure of Lenny McLean, bare knuckle boxer, bouncer, actor and author

the service in Stratford, east London   PHOTOGRAPHS: SEAN SMITH

BARE KNUCKLE boxer, nightclub enforcer, actor and best-selling author Lenny McLean was today being given the East End's version of a state funeral.

McLean — known as "The Guv'nor" and the veteran of some 3,000 brutal and illegal brawls — was being sent off by East End royalty and his newer friends from the world of showbusiness.

Ironically McLean, who died aged 49, had been a prominent mourner at the last big East London funeral for his friend Ronnie Kray three years ago.

Today McLean's send-off did not draw onlookers in their thousands as Kray's had, but the trappings were the same, as were many of the guests.

Four black-plumed horses waited in Hoxton Street to draw the coffin carrying McLean's huge six-foot-three, 20-stone frame through the streets of Hoxton, Shoreditch, Bethnal Green and Stratford — which had been his manor — to the City of London Crematorium in Leytonstone.

Behind the horse-drawn hearse a cortege of black limousines, draped in floral tributes, followed along with police motorcycle outriders.

More piles of flowers — many simply dedicated to "The Guv'nor" — mounted up in front of the funeral directors and spilled over to the pie and mash shop next door. Bulky security men in black suits and ties, with shaven and tattooed heads, looked on as the guests, including former gangster Tony

by JOHN STURGIS

Lambrianou, ex-page three girl Maureen Flanigan and football hardman Vinnie Jones assembled.

The latter was a newer acquaintance from his third career as an actor. Earlier there were the bare-knuckle fights — backroom affairs in which the only rule was that the fight was over when one man could no longer fight back. Even this rule was sometimes violated: McLean first came to prominence when a television documentary showed him stamping on an unconscious opponent.

After some 3,000 fights and £200,000 in prize money, McLean was able to brag that he had never lost. "I wouldn't allow that," he said.

Then there were the nightclub bouncer years, when he dished out punishment to clubbers with too little respect at establishments from the Camden Palace to Glasgow.

In the end, it was the death of a clubber at the Hippodrome in 1991 — McLean was cleared of murder but sentenced to 18 months for GBH — that saw him turn away from violence to acting after a meeting with Mike Reid, who plays Frank the secondhand car dealer in EastEnders.

He was asked to write memoirs of a "career" in which he was twice shot and stabbed. McLean died of cancer last month — the day before The Guv'nor was published.

ckle fighter

man — if you weren't facing him in the ring."

Tony Lambrianou, a member of the Krays' gang who was jailed for 15 years in 1969 for his part in the murder of Jack "The Hat" McVitie, said: "It seems all the proper people are dying off. It's coming to the end of the line."

Helen Keating, of the television series London's Burning, said he was "a larger than life character". Many of the flowers in front of the funeral parlour referred to "The Guv'nor" or "Daddy Cool".

Charlie Richardson, the gangster who was jailed for 25

years for grievous bodily harm, was among mourners waiting at the City of London crematorium, in Stratford. The funeral limousines, with their floral messages from McLean's wife, Val, and children, Kelly and Jamie, followed the hearse.

A friend, John Huntley, likened McLean to the legendary old prize-fighters John L Sullivan and Jack Dempsey. In his book, McLean himself wrote that, despite his dangerous life, he never considered his days might be numbered. But, suddenly it was "bosh, it's all over".

Helen Weathers at the funeral of the bare-knuckle bruiser who turned his life around too late

AS THE casket was lifted from the funeral carriage drawn by six plumed horses, the hard men bowed their heads.

Tough men with thick necks and names like Alfie, Nosher and Sammy. Hard-eyed men in smart black suits and gold chains who preferred not to give their names at all.

Kray gang member Tony Lambrianou stood shoulder to shoulder with top brass gangsters like Charlie Richardson and Mad Frankie Fraser.

They had come to pay their last respects to The Guv'nor, the man they regarded as the hardest of them all.

Lenny McLean, the legendary bare-knuckle boxer, was being given the sort of send-off London's East End reserves for its finest.

They were all there to say good-bye to the man who'd exchanged a brutal notoriety for more conventional fame as an actor in the hit series *The Knock*.

Even soccer's hard man Vinnie Jones, who stars with Lenny in the hit movie *Lock, Stock And Two Smoking Barrels*, looked humbled by the occasion.

This was a man who'd never lost one of his 3,000 violent, vicious fights, only to be beaten in the end by cancer, the one thing he couldn't knock into submission.

Yesterday, his widow Val, 47, his two children Jamie, 26 and Kelly, 25, were joined by boxers and celebrities to give the cockney giant a send-off worthy of his reputation as a hardman with a heart of gold.

As Les Martin, representing Charlie Kray at the funeral, put it: "If Ronnie Kray has opened a nightclub in Heaven, Lenny's on the gate." Hundreds of mourners packed into the chapel at the City of London crematorium in Manor Park for the service.

Lenny's widow Val, his wife of more than 30 years, wept as Stevie Wonder's hit *The Greatest Love Of All* was played at the end of the hour-long service.

Afterwards people queued to pay tribute to Lenny. Vinnie Jones said: "He was like an uncle to us all. He was a tough man but I was privileged to see his softer side on many occasions."

Maureen Flanagan, who in 1971 was the first Page Three girl, recalled Lenny's gentleness with women and his quick wit.

She said: "His sense of humour was terrific and he was a good family man. He loved his wife, he loved his kids.

"He was a fighting man but he did his fighting in the ring, whether bare-knuckled or with gloves."

Former *London's Burning* star Craig Fairbrass, who is currently starring in *Duck Patrol* and was going to play Lenny in a film of his life said: "He was a natural actor. Landing his first acting part gave him the chance to start the kind of life he always wanted.

"It's such a shame that he died just as he got his first big breakthrough. He never lived long enough to see his new movie released."

Lenny's life was more dramatic than any TV or film script.

BORN 49 years ago in Hoxton, one of the toughest areas of London, he'd grown up with violence. By the age of 10 his jaw had been broken twice by his stepfather.

By 15 he'd been sacked from his first proper job after beating up his foreman. Spells in Borstal and approved schools did not put him off a career spent firmly on the edge of the law.

In his autobiography, *The Guv'nor* — which he never lived to see top the best seller charts — he wrote: "It was a rough part of London and violence was all I ever knew, not love."

A bouncer in some of London's toughest clubs, 20-stone Lenny thought nothing of taking on 18 thugs at once. He even put nine of them in hospital.

To supplement his income he drifted into bare-knuckle fights and unlicensed boxing.

With his 54-inch chest, 40-inch waist, 20-inch neck and an awesome reputation for violence it is a wonder that anyone was prepared to take him on.

But 3,000 did — and 3,000 lost.

He'd had his hands broken 15 times and his nose smashed more times than he cared to remember.

But in the old East End tradition he always maintained that he only ever hit people he thought deserved it — or those mad enough to take him on.

He was jailed for 18 months in 1983 for grievous bodily harm, but turned his back on fighting after a

FINAL ROUND: Fitting tribute for L

RESPECT: Vinnie Jones

sensational court case four years ago when he was accused of murder.

He had been arrested after he admitted punching 31-year-old Gary Humphreys in the Hippodrome night-club in central London. Humphreys later died after choking on his own blood.

Lenny was cleared of murder but served 18 months for actual

bodil
becar
feren
EastE
to ac

He
whei
smug
Kno
look
on
com

BRUTAL: Lenny never lost a fight

LENNY THE LEGACY

Pictures by ROGER ALLEN, ARNOLD SLATER, ALISDAIR MACDONALD and BILL ROWNTREE

, inset, whose hard-man reputation launched his acting career

from Lenny's wife and children

ide he
w a dif-
neeting
turned

eer and
art of
in *The*
en you
rd men
poofs
nave to

act tough. I'm tough without trying." Paul Knight, producer of *The Knock*, who was present at yesterday's funeral said: "He was an absolute natural.

"He was larger than life and became a mascot on *The Knock*. He often spoke about how acting gave him the second chance that he was looking for.

"But he was still a scary per-

son. I for one, wouldn't have liked to get on the wrong side of him." Lenny's agent Chuck Julian added: "It's tragic that Lenny survived the life he had and was on the way to major success.

"As big as he was in size it didn't compare with how big his heart was — certainly to his friends, if not his enemies."

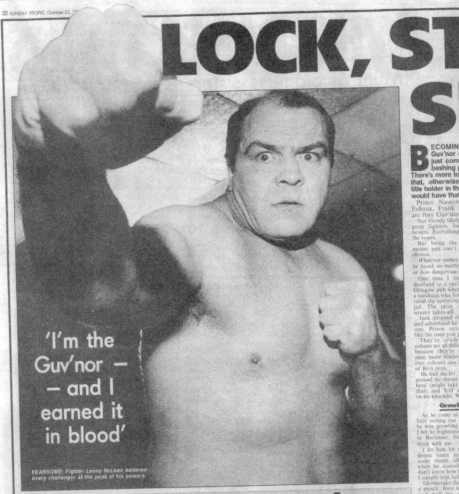

LOCK, STO
SM

BECOMING the Guv'nor doesn't just come from bashing people. There's more to it than that, otherwise every title holder in the world would have that name.

Prince Naseem, Chris Eubank, Frank Bruno — are they Guv'nors?

Not bloody likely! They're great fighters, but they're boxers. Everything stops at the ropes.

But being the Guv'nor means you can't pick and choose.

Whatever comes up has to be faced, no matter how bad or how dangerous.

One time I travelled to Scotland to a yard behind a Glasgow pub where I fought a hardman who for years had ruled the notorious Barlinnie jail. The prize, £16,000 winner takes all.

Jock stripped off his shirt and advertised he was an ex-con. Prison tattoos are like the ones you get outside.

They're crude and the colours are all different shades because they're done with pins, razor blades and whatever colours can be dug out of Biro pens.

He had the lot. Dotted around the throat saying 'Sign here' (might take him up on that), and 'Kill' and 'Dr...' on his knuckles. What an...

Growling

As he came at me he had hate oozing out of him and he was growling like a... I bet he frightened everyone in Barlinnie, but it didn't work with me.

I let him hit me about a dozen times just to some steam off, and when he started think... don't know how to thre... I caught him full on the...

Gloves take the sting out a punch. Bare knuckles and half his ear fl... down, leaking blood a... him. I don't think he... because he came back... left and a right, both ve...

I stepped back and ... him in the knee cap. ... feel me big toe snap, ... he's gone down on his knee and half swung a ... knuckled him in the kil... hard as I could hit...

He went down po... but I continued to ba... until he lay still. The ... half a dozen people jum... me and dragged me a... arms and legs think... still fighting but thos... have got a tight grip...

I watched as I... rolled on to his bac... wasn't moving at x... thing I knew we wer... doing 100mph tow...

Everyone looked up to Lenny

FOOTBALLER Vinnie Jones, who co-starred with Lenny in the film Lock, Stock And Two Smoking Barrels, says: "Lenny commanded respect from everyone on the set, from the tea girls to the big actors. His motto on the set was 'Respect people and be respected.'

"I remember we all had a football match at the end of filming Lock... and Lenny said 'Don't pass the ball to me, Vinnie, I can't breathe'. He didn't look well, but I was devastated when I heard he had terminal cancer. He was like an uncle to everyone. Lenny was a lovely guy."

Former London's Burning star Craig Fairbrass, who is to play Lenny in a film based on his life, says: "I knew Lenny off-and-on for 12 years. I first met him

when he attended a party for my film Queen & Country.

"Lenny looked like he'd been built for nothing other than fighting. He had the build, the hands, the neck, even the voice.

"I saw Lenny fight a couple of times, and the guy was amazing. What surprised me most was how quick he was, he had the speed you normally only associate with someone half his size.

"Even when I first met Lenny there was talk of playing him in a film. He was convinced immediately I should play him, which I'll always be grateful for."

Comedian Freddie Starr says: "I'll never forget my first meeting with Lenny. I knew how tough he was, but I wasn't frightened because everyone who knew

Lenny would tell you he was never a bully. I needed some business attending to, which required Lenny's help but I arrived three hours late for our meeting.

"I didn't find out until later that Lenny was ready to give me a right telling-off. I told Lenny the truth and said, 'I've been up all night with a bird.'

"I knew Lenny was a fan, and reckoned the only way to redeem myself was to make a joke of it so I'd taken along a pair of joke eyes which looked really bloodshot.

"I'd covered my eyes while apologising and then took my hands away so the eyes came out on springs. Lenny fell about laughing, and we never had a cross word after that."

STAND-IN: Fairbrass

'I'm the Guv'nor — — and I earned it in blood'

FEARSOME: Fighter Lenny McLean battered every challenger at the peak of his powers

254

SUNDAY PEOPLE, October 25, 1998   33

CK AND TWO
OKING FISTS

HARD AND SOFT: Lenny (above left) in Lock, Stock... and (right) with wife Val

...ection in the TV series The Knock

TOUGH-GUY Lenny McLean was Britain's top bare knuckle fighter for 20 years. They called him The Guv'nor.

Now the hard man, star of this year's hit movie Lock, Stock And Two Smoking Barrels, has hit even greater fame AFTER his death.

Lenny was a king of the London Underworld but now — three months after he died — he has been catapulted to national fame with his best-selling and acclaimed auto-biography The Guv'nor.

Lenny also had a promising career as an actor. He played a bootlegger in ITV's Customs thriller The Knock. But he was beaten at the age of 49 for the first time in his life — by cancer. Now, in death, he has achieved the stardom he craved. After his funeral The Guv'nor shot to No.1 in the best-seller list and is still in the top 10.

Scripts are being drawn up for a movie in which he will be played by ex-London's Burning star Craig Fairbrass.

Today, for the first time he tells you in his own words just what he really had to do to earn the title of The Guv'nor, an accolade that meant so much to him.

It's shocking, it's scary...and it's brutal. But it makes gripping and sensational reading...

's hardest man hits fame in death

...wanted ...doing. ...second ...ess on. ...funny ...d been ...r after ...k I've ...getting ...g is in ...and ...e are ...t gets ...ener - ...ht and ...tch as ...er get. ...where ...goug- ...e that ...your ...ribs ...ers are ...w and ...But ...thinks ...s that ...t. not ...few ...rs put ...lenge ...never ...t in a ...e title- ...Pretty ...mself

as the hardest man in England. Prison officers had beaten Shaw around the head with truncheons so often he had more scars than hair.

He's the only person I've ever heard of who has ever smashed his way through a locked prison cell door.

He was The Mean Machine, the toughest unlicensed fighter in Britain.

To become the Guv'nor I had to take his crown.

I'd been training for weeks, including putting a rope around my waist, tying it to the bumper of a Mini and dragging the car around the park, for our fight at a theatre in North London.

Pumping

The bell goes and he tears at me, his arms going like pistons. He's trying to finish me quick.

I don't know if you've had a fight as an adult, but if you haven't then let me mark your card.

The average person couldn't sustain a real fight for much more than a minute.

Adrenaline is pumped into your body for the off but it's short-lived. Then you're left drained out.

Shaw gets about four good belts in but two of mine send him backwards and I keep going with the left and rights to the body.

A surprised look flickered across his face and he went down. He got back up, but now he's on the defensive. I've got him.

I battered him full circuit of the ring, then as he gave me two feeble jabs he wasn't quick enough with his guard and I chopped him to the side of his head.

Roy was spark out. His team dragged him to his feet and pulled him into the corner and as he came to he was trying to carry on.

I could hear his second shouting. 'It's over Roy, it's over.'

I swung round to the crowd. They're going wild.

I held my arms high and shouted to them all: 'Who's the Guv'nor?' a great cheer went up around the place.

Again I threw my arms in the air and bellowed out: 'Who's the Guv'nor?'

The roar was deafening 'Lenny, Lenny, Lenny' everybody's on their feet.

My mob's going crazy and even Roy's lot are clapping and cheering. I've done it.

I never really set out to be the Guv'nor but now I was and nobody would ever take that away from me.

In the dressing room afterwards, I'm sitting having a cup of coffee after my couple of minutes' effort and I look up and two fellers walk in.

I recognised them but couldn't place their faces.

Then the penny dropped

and I went: "F*** me, it's Superman." They both laughed and introduced them-selves — Christoper Reeve and Gene Hackman.

Can you believe it, these two superstars wanted me to sign a programme for them?

They congratulated me on my win. I was gobsmacked

So now I'm the Guv'nor.

I carried on with my other job as a minder. I didn't go looking for violence but some-times came to me.

When I went looking for it, fighting with bare knuckles on the cobbles at fairs and gipsy camps or with gloves in the ring, I was doing it for my family — it paid well and gave them a good life.

Tough

I took on very tough men, a lot of them bigger than me, so I wasn't taking liberties. They knew what they were up against and accepted it.

An old guy I'd become friends with asked me to visit him at his home in Canterbury, Kent, to discuss a proposition.

He met me at the door of his great big house.

He's got a dressing gown on and looks like your grandad.

But this 70-year-old Amer-ican-Italian is a semi-retired Mafia Don.

If you saw him, you'd want to help him across the road.

We have lunch then he digs out the brandy and cigars. He

says: "I was talking to one of the family in New York. I told him that in this country we have the toughest street fighter I've ever seen.

"The family have a cham-pion by the name of John Mc-Cormack who is also unbeatable.

"I want you to go to New York and show him he's very wrong

"Everything is arranged, even your purse, £14,000 plus expenses."

A week later we're on our way. I took a pal of mine who is a high-flier in the straight world now and his clients might get a bit fidgety finding out who he's mixed with in his past.

We were staying at the New York Plaza. Posh suites each, everything on the Family slate.

The guys we were dealing with took us out for a meal.

These guys run most of the business in New York. Forget the Mayor, forget the police. Funny though, no dark glasses, no menace, just four businessmen.

Next day we were driven out to a huge warehouse.

McCormack was 6ft 5ins and 24 stone give or take a pound. He's stamping up and down and punching one clenched fist into the palm of the other over and over again.

All the suits are there. There's one light bulb above our heads and most of the

four rib-breakers into him. Rattled him.

The atmosphere was dead quiet. Too serious for a bit of cheering.

He looks beaten, but he's not.

Whoop - look out he comes at me like a bull.

I've side-stepped, clenched my fists together and smashed him in the kidneys.

He's fallen on to his hands. Six punches to the jaw, cheek and forehead finished him.

Blood was pouring from his injuries making a little pool beside his head.

Funny really, I've smashed the Family's best and you'd think there'd be a bit of a fuss but there was no reaction at all.

The suits handed over a briefcase with the money, wished us well and were gone.

Never even looked at their man laying flat on the deck, bleeding and still spark out.

We got back to London without any problems.

I squared my pal with a few grand, got my hands plastered up and went home.

I gave my wife Val the money and went upstairs to lay on the bed.

When she brought me up a cup of tea she was cry-ing: "Oh Len, I wish you'd give up fighting, the strain's doing my head in."

I gave her a kiss and cuddle and said: "Doll, its a hard game but it don't half beat cleaning windows. I'd have to wash and polish Crystal Palace twice to earn the sort of money I've just picked up."

© The Guv'nor by Lenny McLean with Peter Gerrard, published by Blake Publishing, price £14.99. Adaptation by MIKE RIDLEY.

255

Friends line streets to say farewell to the Guv'nor

● *Lenny McLean went on to become the most fearsome fighter in Britain – cancer was the only opponent to beat him.*

BRITAIN'S hardest man, Hoxton-born Lenny McLean, was remembered as his funeral procession passed through Hackney yesterday (Wednesday).

Residents lined the route to pay their respects to the iron-fisted 49-year-old who died of lung cancer last week.

The procession, led by a horse-drawn hearse, began in Hoxton Street only yards from where Lenny grew up in Gopsall Road. It went down Whitmore, Downham and Kingsland Roads before turning into Bethnal Green and onto the City of London Crematorium in Manor Park.

It was east London's largest funeral since Ronnie Kray died two years ago.

Lenny earned the title the Guv'nor after beating the previous toughest man in Britain – Roy "Mean Machine" Shaw.

The 6ft 3in giant became a folk hero after an undefeated career of 3,000 bare-knuckle fights. In one he bit through

● *The boy who would be The Guv'nor. A picture from Lenny McLean's book shows him (second from left) as a youngster in Hoxton. He also lived in Kent Street, Haggerston.*

his opponent's windpipe. He was diagnosed with terminal lung cancer this spring.

Lenny leaves behind two children Jamie and Kelly. Lenny's story is told in the new Blake hardback The Guv'nor, available in bookshops priced £14.99.

Bestsellers

Two tough guys slugging it out at the top of the hardback charts this week. Lenny "the Guv'nor" McLean has reached number one with his bruising autobiography, knocking out previous titleholder Alexander "the Great", faltering now that his TV run has ended. Despite mixed reviews, David Ewing Duncan's The Cal-

endar has entered the chart at number three and is likely to rise with radio exposure this week.

Elsewhere among the hardbacks, there are some odd rises by books one had assumed were drifting downwards. Christopher Reeve's Still Me: A Life has climbed up to 11; Nick Hornby's About A Boy is back at 20; Julie

Burchill's Diana is rising again at 47; and Birthday Letters by Ted Hughes OM has moved up to 56. Brian Johnston's Letters Home — letters Johnners wrote as a schoolboy to his mother — is at 31, proving that cricket-lovers will buy just about anything, and there is the happy conjunction of Mary Warnock's The Intelligent

Person's Guide to Ethics at 22 and Bart Simpson's Guide to Life by Matt Groening at 25. Which will be your vade mecum?

In the paperback chart, Irvine Welsh has maintained a healthy lead. The other paperback original to make the top 10 is Jane Green's Jemima J, another of those twentysomething tales

that mix sex, romance and dieting, not necessarily in that order. Like Helen Fielding, Green's background is in journalism; this is her second novel. According to the press release that accompanied the book, she will be married in January: a happy day for her and an unmissable novel scenario for her publisher.

Top 10 UK hardbacks

	Last week	Weeks	RRP
1 The Guv'nor L. McLean & P Gerrard (Blake)	2	3	£14.99
2 In the Footsteps of Alexander the Great Michael Wood (BBC)	1	4	£17.99
3 The Calendar David Ewing Duncan (4th Estate)			£12.99
4 Harry Potter and the Chamber of Secrets Joanne Rowling (Bloomsbury)	3	7	£10.99
5 Thesaurus of English Words and Phrases Peter Roget (Penguin Press)	4	3	£14.99
6 The Man Who Loved Only Numbers Paul Hoffman (Fourth Estate)	9	2	£12.99
7 Pears Cyclopedia 1998-99 ed. C Cook (Penguin)			£16.59
8 The Last Continent: Discworld Series Terry Pratchett (Doubleday)	6	15	£16.59
9 Klone and I Danielle Steele (Bantam)	5	1	£9.99
10 Stalingrad Antony Beevor (Viking)	7	14	£25

Mass-market paperbacks

	Last week	Weeks	RRP
1 Filth Irvine Welsh (Cape)	1	2	£9.99
2 The God of Small Things Arundhati Roy (Flamingo)	2	15	£6.99
3 Enduring Love Ian McEwan (Vintage)	3	7	£6.99
4 Memoirs of a Geisha Arthur Golden (Vintage)	4	11	£6.99
5 Captain Corelli's Mandolin Louis de Bernières (Minerva)	5	52	£6.99
6 Bridget Jones's Diary: A Novel Helen Fielding (Picador)	9	59	£5.99
7 Angela's Ashes: A Memoir of a Childhood Frank McCourt (Flamingo)	6	64	£7.99
8 The Little Book of Calm Paul Wilson (Penguin)		75	£1.99
9 Falling Leaves Return to their Roots Adeline Yen Mah (Penguin)	8	23	£6.99
10 Jemima J Jane Green (Penguin)	14	–	£5.99

Original paperback fiction

	Last week	Weeks	RRP
1 Filth Irvine Welsh (Cape)	1	2	£9.99
2 My Legendary Girlfriend Mike Gayle (Sceptre)	2	3	£10
3 The Sopranos Alan Warner (Cape)	3	10	£8.99
4 Venus Envy Louise Bagshawe (Orion)	6	3	£9.99
5 Intimacy Hanif Kureishi (Faber)	7	15	£9.99
6 The Talk of the Town Ardal O'Hanlon (Sceptre)	4	13	£10
7 At All Costs John Gilstrap (Michael Joseph)	8	1	£10
8 My Year of Meat Ruth L Ozeki (Picador)	9	6	£9.99
9 Eleven Hours Paullina Simons (Flamingo)			£9.99
10 England Away John King (Cape)	5	16	£9.99

Information supplied by Whitaker Booktrack based on sales in more than 2,000 high-street bookshops

Bart Simpson ...read my book, or else